"The authors of this powerful, pioneering work show therapists essential but often invisible themes of work with Jewish women, and they edify all people through their poignant, witty, courageous personal stories about how it feels to be doubly or multiply oppressed. Reading this, we all become more richly human and humane; we are urged to think carefully and are moved to feel deeply and warmly."

Paula J. Caplan, PhD, CPsych, Author of *Don't Blame Mother* and *The Myth of Women's Masochism;* Professor of Applied Psychology, Ontario Institute for Studies in Education, University of Toronto, Toronto, Ontario, Canada

"I'm moved by the women who have written *Jewish Women in Therapy.* All of the contributors—from lesbian feminist therapists to heterosexual poets to professors of linguistics—are Jewish women trying to find the felt imperatives of Judaism in their feminism and to balance ethics and tradition in their praxis."

Martha Roth, AB, Editor, *Hurricane Alice;* Vice President, National Writer's Union, Minneapolis, Minnesota

"This is a long overdue book and the first of its kind. Useful, interesting, exciting, and necessary."

Phyllis Chesler, PhD, Professor, The College of Staten Island, City University of New York; Author of *Women and Madness, About Men,* and *Sacred Bond: The Legacy of Baby M.*

Jewish Women in Therapy: Seen But Not Heard

Jewish Women in Therapy: Seen But Not Heard

Edited by
Rachel Josefowitz Siegel and Ellen Cole

Jewish Women in Therapy: Seen But Not Heard was simultaneously issued by The Haworth Press, Inc., under the same title, as a special issue of *Women & Therapy*, Volume 10, Number 4 1990, Rachel Josefowitz Siegel and Ellen Cole, Editors.

Harrington Park Press
New York • London

ISBN 0-918393-93-0

Published by

Harrington Park Press, 10 Alice Street, Binghamton, NY 13904-1580
EUROSPAN/Harrington, 3 Henrietta Street, London WC2E 8LU England

Harrington Park Press is a subsidiary of the Haworth Press, Inc., 10 Alice Street, Binghamton, NY 13904-1580.

Jewish Women in Therapy: Seen But Not Heard was originally published as *Women & Therapy*, Volume 10, Number 4 1990.

Cover design by Marshall Andrews.

Library of Congress Cataloging-in-Publication Data

Jewish women in therapy : seen but not heard / edited by rachel Josefowitz Siegel and Ellen Cole.
    p. cm.
    "Simultaneously issued by the Haworth Press, Inc., under the same title, as a special issue of Women & therapy, volume 10, number 4 1990.
    Includes bibliographical references.
    ISBN 0-918393-93-0 (acid free paper)
    1. Women, Jewish—Mental health. 2. Women, Jewish—Counseling of. 3. Psychotherapy.
I. Siegel, Rachel Josefowitz. II. Cole, Ellen.
RC451.5.J4J49   1990
616.89'14'082—dc20   90-5384
                                                                                          CIP

CONTENTS

∞ ALL HARRINGTON PARK PRESS BOOKS
ARE PRINTED ON CERTIFIED
ACID-FREE PAPER

ABOUT THE EDITORS

Rachel Josefowitz Siegel, MSW, a Jewish feminist activist, is a clinical social worker in private practice in Ithaca, New York. A founding member of the Feminist Therapy Institute, she writes, lectures, and conducts workshops on Jewish women, women over 60, and counteracting negative biases and oppressions. She also co-edited with Joan Hamerman Robbins the book *Women Changing Therapy: New Assessments, Values, and Strategies in Feminist Therapy* (The Haworth Press, 1983).

Ellen Cole, PhD, has devoted more than 25 years to the practice of psychology. She is a faculty member in the Human Development Program, Prescott College, Prescott, Arizona, and an AASECT certified sex therapist and sex educator. In addition, she co-edited, with Esther Rothblum, the book *Another Silenced Trauma*, which received a 1987 Distinguished Publication Award from the Association for Women in Psychology. Dr. Cole is a co-editor of the journal *Women & Therapy* and of the Haworth Series on Women.

In Memory of Benjamin M. Siegel

Preface

When Jewish women are seen in therapy, the significance of their Jewishness is often not recognized. Even Jewish clients themselves may not be aware of its impact on their lives. The purpose of this volume, then, is to examine the important and pervasive effects of being brought up female and Jewish, so that Jewish women in therapy will be both seen and heard.

This volume is a beginning. It is the first collection of articles, ever, to focus on issues of Jewish women in the context of counseling and psychotherapy. The idea emerged on the way home from the 1989 conference of the Association for Women in Psychology. A Jewish caucus had been born there; the energy and enthusiasm were inspirational. A computer search of existing literature revealed only one article on our topic (Siegel, 1986). Our aim, as it developed from that point on, has been to convey the richness and variety of Jewish women's experiences, the Jewishness and femaleness of the concerns, issues, values, and attitudes that Jewish women — clients and therapists — bring into the therapy room. To honor the variety of expression among Jewish women, we have respected each author's spelling or transliteration of Jewish terms.

It has been an exciting process as each of us has responded to the challenge and the opportunity to be heard as Jewish women. Laura S. Brown, Adrienne J. Smith, and Kayla Wiener, all experienced feminist therapists, have not previously written specifically about Jewish issues. Rita Arditti, Evelyn Torton Beck, Susannah Heschel, and Melanie Kaye/Kantrowitz have introduced Jewish women's issues into contemporary feminist literature. Here they focus for the first time on mental health implications. Amy Sheldon writes from her own Jewish woman's experience; Susan L. Steinberg examines her work with a psychotic patient through a Jewish woman's lens; Mira J. Spektor and Miriam L. Vogel contribute a poetic dimension to understanding the impact of the Holocaust on our lives. Betsy Giller and Rachel Aber Schlesinger, using data from their graduate school research, report on their work with particular groups of Jewish women.

Each article opened the door to further questions and ideas, to a desire for more in-depth inquiry, for wishing there was space for additional topics and concerns. We would have liked to include articles on Holocaust survivors and their daughters, mental health issues of recent Jewish Soviet immigrant women, Orthodox Jewish women, poor Jewish women and rich ones. We can imagine articles on the therapeutic implications of newly emerging Jewish rituals, on our emotional response to the political situation in Israel, on our efforts to understand and communicate the multiple oppressions of all women. And yet this collection is full and varied as it stands. We hope it will also stimulate future writing. It is a beginning.

Rachel's Statement

On a very personal level, since the editing of this volume coincided with the immensely sad and stressful period of my husband's final illness, I would like, some day when there is more distance from the pain, to write about the experience of death and mourning from the Jewish woman's perspective. I am deeply grateful to have shared my life with Benjamin M. Siegel, a man whose dedication to all that is Jewish was matched by his respect for women; he was open, after some persuasion, to the need for feminist analysis and change within Jewish custom and observance as well as within our own family. I am also glad to recognize that the current wave of feminist activism within the Jewish community has had an impact on my own Jewish congregation. As a new widow, my grieving need not be exacerbated by the traditional exclusion of women from communal rituals. My daughter and I are not dependent on my sons for saying kaddish* as we would have been 20 years ago; we have established our right to speak our own prayer and to stand up and be counted when ten Jews are needed for a minyan.**

---

*kaddish—the prayer for the departed that is recited at every service by immediate members of the family; traditionally only by men.

**minyan—a congregation of ten Jews needed to recite certain prayers including the kaddish; traditionally only men can be counted for a minyan.

Ellen's Statement

My Jewish parents, like many of their contemporaries, were atheists and anti-religionists. I received no formal training in Jewish traditions, was not allowed to stay home from our New York City public school on Jewish holidays (I remember many days when my brother and I were the only ones there), have now lived for nearly three decades in overwhelmingly "gentile" towns (Plainfield, Vermont and Prescott, Arizona), and to this day do not know, with certainty, why Passover or Hanukah are celebrated. And yet I know, as deeply as I know anything, that I am a Jewish woman. When Rachel suggested we co-edit a volume about Jewish women and mental health, I was enthusiastic but insecure. This has not been one of my areas of specialization. But as our work progressed, I experienced a deep satisfaction from reconnecting with my heritage. It has reminded me that as women, as feminists, as Jews, we come in all varieties; the differences and the connections are profound.

Rachel Josefowitz Siegel
Ellen Cole

REFERENCE

Siegel, R.J. (1986). Antisemitism and sexism in stereotypes of Jewish women. *Women and Therapy*, 5(2/3), 249-257.

Introduction:
Jewish Women in Therapy:
Seen But Not Heard

Rachel Josefowitz Siegel

Maasu even habonim
haita le rosh pina
The stone which the builders rejected
has become the chief corner-stone. (Psalm 118:22)

One of my favorite phrases in the prayerbook, the words keep running through my head as I think about Jewish women.

Too often have the builders and leaders of Jewish ritual and Jewish community excluded and ridiculed us. Too often have non-Jews misjudged us. Too often have feminists seen only our privileges and dismissed our pains. We have been frequently unaware of our Jewish sisters when they do not fit our limited views of what a Jewish woman should be. We have been embarassed, ashamed or uncomfortable with that part of ourselves that we perceive as being too Jewish or not Jewish enough. Our therapists have more often than not ignored the historical and political realities of our Jewish heritage, dismissed our oppression as Jews and as women and devalued

---

Rachel Josefowitz Siegel is a Jewish feminist activist, a clinical social worker in private practice in Ithaca, NY and a founding member of the Feminist Therapy Institute. She writes, lectures and does workshops on Jewish women, women over sixty and counteracting negative biases and oppressions. She also co-edited with Joan Hamerman Robbins, *Women Changing Therapy: New Assessments, Values and Strategies in Feminist Therapy*; Women & Therapy, Volume 2, Nos. 2/3, 1983.

The author wishes to thank Paula J. Caplan for her generous support and feedback, also Nina J. Katz and Jude Keith for their assistance.

1

the Jewish flavor of our lifestyle. The issues of Jewish women have not been part of our own training as therapists or of our professional discourse and literature.

When Jewish women are ignored, misperceived, ridiculed, excluded and rejected, we begin to feel confused about who we really are. We may feel conflicted about being Jewish and being female. Our vision becomes distorted, our tears dry into pillars of salt, something within us turns to stone. Yet we manage to carry on; like rocks we develop an inner strength of our own and a beauty of many shapes and colors. We do not allow ourselves to be so easily discarded. We become survivors, tough and resilient like the harsh desert landscape of the Negev.

Jewish women who do not fit the idealized stereotype of the happily married and Jewishly observant mother of Jewish sons, nevertheless have a 'Yiddishe neshome,' a Jewish soul. We need to start naming and appreciating our Jewish traits. We need to reclaim the power to speak our Jewish women's voices within the Jewish community and within feminist circles, as well as in the world at large.

In this collection we give voice, for the first time in the literature of psychotherapy, to the mental health issues and concerns of Jewish women. Our goal has been to draw attention to the many ways of being a Jewish woman in America today and to the rich variety of Jewish women's experiences, concerns and life styles, all in less than 200 pages. We have wanted both to celebrate the contributions of Jewish women to feminism and to therapy and also to convey the complexities of our oppression, for these two aspects of being Jewish and female co-exist in our society.

Yes, we have been rejected and yes, we have become chief corner stones. We have been silenced by our traditional position within Judaism, and by the anti-Semitic and male-centered aspects of our environment. Yet we dare to speak up on the most vital issues of our times. Much like our non-Jewish sisters, we are the central figures, the activists, the silent helpers, the always available listeners, fixers, nurturers within our families, our communities, our political movements, our professional organizations. Our leadership is becoming more vocal, more overt.

We have also been maligned and misdiagnosed, both when we are relegated to marginal status and when we are performing tasks of central importance. We have been called Jewish mothers and Jewish princesses with derision instead of respect. We are the women whose strength and valor are constantly exaggerated into overly benign or overly malevolent caricatures. Yet we have become the doers, often at the forefront of radical thought and social change.

Jewish women in our time are not only seen, we are beginning to be heard. Our voices are emerging in scholarly discourse and in political debate; in many congregations we now participate fully in religious rituals that had traditionally been the exclusive domain of Jewish men. Our voices are, however, still far from being accepted by all or welcomed by the majority.

This past year, for the first time in Jewish history, a group of Jewish women of every religious and secular persuasion have been meeting regularly in Jerusalem, for communal prayer at the Wailing Wall.* The brave 'Women of the Wall' have been harassed and yelled at by Jewish men and women who object to the organized presence of women at this holy place of worship; they have had stones thrown at them by ultra-orthodox Jews and have been denied permission to carry a Sefer Torah,** to read from it and even to pray as a group in the separate and unequal women's section.

Closer to home, Jewish women are being called too loud and too pushy. "JAP" baiting has spread throughout college campuses. Among therapists and other mental health workers, we have been seen but not heard; we have been present in fairly large numbers and presented our research and ideas on many subjects, yet we have hardly ever spoken, written or presented papers on the issues of Jewish women.

We have the immense privilege of living in a period of profound and fundamental changes within Judaism and in our world. These changes are radical as well as much too slow. We experience

---

Wailing Wall—or 'western wall,' last remnant of the Temple mount; the site of pilgrimage and prayer. Women are permitted only at the small women's section and are not permitted to form a minyan or to perform the Torah service.

**Sefer Torah*—scrolls of holy scripture containing the Pentateuch or Five Books of Moses. A section of the Torah is read, traditionally only by men, during Sabbath and Holy Day services.

change and the need for change within ourselves and in our relationships; we are troubled when we long for it and deeply affected when we witness, participate, initiate, follow or resist it. We bring our doubts, hesitations and exultations into the therapy room. In this volume Jewish women begin to talk and write about the importance of including the Jewishness of our experience into our therapeutic encounters.

The Generation of Survivors

*In Memory of Eliazer Vogel**

Who I am lies here
buried with the ashes
of those who were not even unknown soldiers

I know that my grandfather Eli
had left a note when sent away by train
to other destinations
his note was found next to the railroad tracks
to Camp Westerbork
he wrote: I'm fine so far; you take care of life

we told one another that he had died
but never talked about the terrible way

names are all over the walls
in memoriam Bergen Belsen
at Mount Sion close to David's Tomb
written in eternal language are messages
of peace and pain
rejoined by an everlasting flame
flickering the dance of death
like the one that brought them here togather
in His Name

there is always Summer outside
consuming like the fire that turned their bones to ashes
the rabbi's helper selling shofars
as a reminder of the prophesies for a day
that might never come

all they are I am
carrier of memories of unknown men and women
brought to life from dust to flesh
as one of a generation of survivors

—Miriam L. Vogel

Miriam Lea Vogel, MSW, is a feminist therapist in private practice in Seattle. Born in Amsterdam, the Netherlands, in 1944, her poetry has been an important way to address the meaning of the Holocaust in her life and the lives of her family and friends. She sees poetry as a part of the therapy and healing process.

*My grandfather Eliazer Vogel died in Sobibor in 1942.

The Issue Is Power:
Some Notes on Jewish Women
and Therapy

Melanie Kaye/Kantrowitz

It begins with power, and why not? Jews are supposed to be all-powerful: controlling Wall Street, the world's money, media, colleges — the world itself. Tucked under the myth of the all-powerful Jew is the victim-Jew, the old-world-Jew, the *shlep*, the *nebish*, and — somber but receding into the vague undifferentiated past — the Holocaust Jew. Riding the myth of the all-powerful Jew is the Israeli, the soldier, the one who breaks the hands of Palestinian children; inherently worse than other soldiers, worse than other men; the one who justifies hatred, is pointed to as proof of the problem: *you see what they're like?*

And the Jewish woman? As a Jew, she's assumed to have so much power already; as a woman, so little that any power she has is excessive. Stereotypes of Jewish women combine with prejudice against powerful women, pressuring us to cloak our strength lest we be seen as pushy; hide our desire, lest we be deemed oversexed (or,

Melanie Kaye/Kantrowitz's work on Jewish, anti-racist, feminist and lesbian themes is widely published, and she has lectured and presented workshops all over the United States and in Canada. She is co-editor of *The Tribe of Dina: A Jewish Women's Anthology* (Boston: Beacon, 1989) and author of *My Jewish Face and Other Stories* (San Francisco: Spinsters/Aunt Lute, 1990). She holds a PhD in Comparative Literature from the University of California at Berkeley, and teaches in the independent study Graduate Program of Vermont College, working with students in the Midwest.

The author is grateful to Judy Chalmer, Michele Clark and Bernice Mennis for critical suggestions and sharing of experience; Michele's expertise as a therapist was particularly helpful. Responsibility for these opinions is mine alone.

fuck on demand, lest we be considered frigid); mute our feelings, lest we be judged overemotional. Jewish lesbians to some extent escape this pressure—we are already displeasing to men, already outside the limits of acceptable female behavior;[1] to some extent, but not entirely. Jewish women are asked to sit on ourselves, lest we seem too . . . too . . .

Too powerful. Too powerful for men, Jews and non-Jews, who consider male dominance their birthright. Too powerful for women, Jews and non-Jews. Often non-Jewish women who are poor, working class or of color, automatically define Jews as privileged, and can only imagine Jewish power being used against them.[2] Often privileged WASP women, raised on politeness and privacy, see Jewish women as *aggressive, bossy, tense, driven, difficult,* not to mention *loud and pushy.* Jewish women, too, depending on the extent of our assimilation and our feelings about our own Jewishness, may respond negatively to strength in other Jewish women. We fear the male/gentile response to that strength. And, loving ourselves insufficiently, trafficking too much in other people's conception of us, we fear our own strength. What will we do with this strength? Make trouble? Hoard privilege? Justify anti-Semitism? Remind us we are Jews?

And the therapist, Jewish or non-Jewish: What is her response to a Jewish woman coming into her strength?

*   *   *

The task of self-love is endless. It is also, for many women, the task of therapy: to learn to love, trust and nurture ourselves, as we were insufficiently loved, trusted and nurtured. But what if a woman has been taught that she is especially selfish, especially unloveable, especially not to be trusted; that she already has too much, takes too much, occupies too much space?

A Jewish woman in the U.S. may well look around to see once poor but now comfortably middle-class relatives saying, *We made it, why can't they?* (Poor Jews, especially women and the elderly, are invisible, disguised by assumptions of Jewish wealth and by the general lack of attention to women and the elderly.) She hears prominent Jews—Jackie Mason, Ed Koch—make horrendous racist statements, while the gritty day-to-day anti-racist work of many

Jews in and out of the Jewish community gets ignored.[3] She reads media hypes about Black-Jewish conflict, dreary rehashed incidents, in which Jews get scapegoated for white racism, and Blacks for Christian and Muslim anti-Semitism. She wants to feel proud of her Jewish tradition, but she finds elements she is not proud of, and it seems this is what non-Jews know best. More feminists know the obscure male prayer that thanks god for not being a woman than any other detail about Judaism. On the one hand, she may feel profoundly threatened by a legacy of hate that haunted, at least, her grandparents; probably her parents; possibly herself. On the other hand, she may feel profoundly ashamed of, and oddly responsible for, the oppression visited by Israelis on Palestinians and masquerading as defense of the Jewish people. About the Holocaust legacy: Is she paranoid or foolishly off guard? About Israel: the same question.

If she moves in progressive circles, she may discover that she cannot say she's a Jew without being called to account for the Israeli army. If she has bothered to educate herself, and point out that armies are armies, and that a huge movement of Israelis oppose their government's policies,[4] she may be shocked by the animosity such a common-sense observation provokes. If she attends a family gathering and offers similar observations, she may be confronted by enraged and terrified relatives who accuse her of not caring about Jews; *You don't know*, they tell her, *you were born here, you're protected*, and often she knows this is true. They say she believes the lies of, strengthens the hands of, her people's enemies.

Either way, she risks anger, dislike, alienation. Either way, it seems as if she is forced to choose. Between being Jewish and being progressive. Between the right and the wrong sides of history. Between her people and the other.

Even a Jew who doesn't identify strongly as Jewish, even if she responds to these scenes, observations, events with bewilderment — *what has this to do with me?* — the question hangs in the air. She may pass as gentile, unconsciously and with no sense of guilt or loss (as in, *my parents were Jewish, but I'm Unitarian*). But assimilated, identified, or, like most Jews in the U.S., somewhere in between, she will grapple with her Jewishness or she will be split from herself.

*   *   *

What is a therapist's task when a Jewish woman becomes her client?

There is a common assumption that Jewishness is an insignificant identity and shouldn't matter — except to those oddball few who practice the religion. A therapist who makes this assumption can damage. Here are some things I want to say to therapists.

Don't assume Jewish identity is unimportant. With Jewish clients, consider the possibility that some blockages relate to alienation from one's Jewish self, and think about how to raise this issue. You work with a woman you could swear is "really" a lesbian; another who claims her working-class background is the past. . . . I assume that most of you have developed strategies for clients like these. Understand that what appears to be a client's casual attitude towards her own Jewishness may be just that, or may mask a loss of which the client is not yet aware, or may protect a tenderness the client feels around her Jewishness because of the common assumption of insignificance.

Don't assume you know how assimilated a given Jewish client is; the woman you know as a radical lesbian carpenter may have spent hours of her childhood in Hebrew school. Ask. Don't assume you know what a given Jewish symbol, holiday, ritual means to your client. A friend tells her therapist she doesn't want to schedule an appointment for Yom Kippur. "What, do you need to pray or something?" cracks the therapist, evoking in my friend feelings of exposure, shame and alienation. Ask a real question. "What does that mean to you?" The first task is not to assume you understand. Assume you need to listen and learn.

Don't assume that Jewishness equals Judaism. Religion is only a part of Jewishness. Jewishness is a peoplehood, a culture, a shared history, an ethnic identity. Conversely, women who struggle to reclaim Judaism are reclaiming not just their religion but their history, their wholeness. That millions died within familial memory for being Jews means that when we go to *shul*, or attend a Jewish event, or wear a star, or long for the sound of Yiddish, Ladino, or Hebrew, or the smell of *tzimes* or *knaidlach*, we are also asserting, *I am a Jew and I am alive*.

Don't assume that reclaiming Jewish identity is simple. Jewishness is an intensely collective endeavor, to be pursued in a community of other Jews. Sometimes the work of re-approaching one's Jewishness involves exploration, the nature of which may well be mysterious even to the explorer. In this work we feel excruciating vulnerability. We feel ashamed for not already knowing tradition, history, culture, language lost to us via assimilation. We feel exposed and foolish for wanting to encompass these things so little seen much less valued by the non-Jewish world. We feel guilty for criticizing family and culture. Besides, given the pain — as well as joy — with which being Jewish has usually bathed our families, our Jewishness is often buried under oceans of tears.

*   *   *

Here are some issues which I believe are especially intense for Jewish women, or have a particularly Jewish slant to them:

Children and Family. The decision to have or not have children, the meaning of family — these issues have particular weight in the Jewish community, as in many other minority communities, especially those subjected to attempted genocide. The people's survival has depended on the strong family, and on the woman's reproductive performance. To take a simple example, the therapist who sees in a Jewish woman's anguish about whether or not to have a child only a classic feminist dilemma may miss a dynamic of which even the client herself may be unaware.

On the other hand, Jewish families are probably as riddled with abuse and dysfunction as other families. Yet there is a myth about the close, happy Jewish family, that Jewish men don't drink or beat their wives or sexually abuse their daughters. These myths make the reality hard to bear for the individual suffering in a non-ideal family. The anguish felt by many women about revealing family secrets is exacerbated by a sense that Jewish families in particular need protection. That we need to be better than the goyim. That by telling the truth we're validating anti-Semitism.

Money. To many non-Jews, Jews *are* money. A friend tells me that whenever she mentions money in therapy sessions she feels intense anxiety, lest her therapist click into anti-Semitic stereotypes. Jews' relationship to money is further complicated by the dramatic class shifts many of us have experienced in our own or in our parents' lifetimes. Add to this a concept of charity deep in the Jewish tradition that is fundamentally different from Christian charity, as the notion of poverty is fundamentally different — neither a blessed state (Catholicism) nor a sign of damnation (Calvinism), but an unfortunate reality to be ameliorated, anonymously and without fanfare, by those who have more.

Alienation. The non-Jewish or assimilated Jewish therapist needs to consider that the woman who looks to her like a "normal white woman" has experienced in her own life or through her parents' experience serious alienation and even danger from being Jewish; Thus the question of Jewish paranoia asserts itself. Many of us were taught that the world is dangerous because the world *is* dangerous. A therapist who treats this fear as pathology seriously misses the point. A friend whose father survived the Holocaust tells of her reluctance to mention Hitler to her therapist; her fear is that her deepest loyalty and rage, her commitment to Jewish survival and memory will be defined as pathology, therapized away.

"The Real Jew." Any minority culture which has encountered the force of American assimilation has lost much of itself. Some Jews have lost more than others, and often we feel ashamed of this loss. Many of us have one Jewish parent, or received no religious education, or have a partner who is not Jewish. From a relatively homogenous culture not so many generations back we have developed a tremendous range of experience and relationships to Jewishness but without a corresponding sense that this range is valid, acceptable. Jews tend to feel judged by other Jews as not Jewish enough; this projection includes our own self-judgment, and makes us either undermine our sense of self or turn from Jewish community, in an effort to avoid this undermining.

*   *   *

To be a Jew is to tangle with history. Even Jews born post-World War II in the U.S. — that is to say, even the most protected Jews the world has known — are formed not only by a personal history that begins at birth but also by the often turbulent experience of our parents and grandparents.

Everyone learns distorted, no longer accurate lessons through parents and other family members. What I am characterizing here as Jewish is the nature and the extent of those lessons.

There's the issue of how to define the self. Traditional therapy focuses on an individual's exploration and healing; its very bias runs counter to the bias of Jewish culture, which is towards the collectivity.[5] Not that the individual should be sacrificed to the community, but that the individual is profoundly connected to the community, so profoundly that separation is not truly possible without extreme loss. In some ways, this stance, deep in the Jewish tradition — as in the tradition of many oppressed peoples — corresponds to feminism.

But even feminist therapists who understand perfectly well that the personal is political, that family and community conflict may be worth probing instead of escaping, who know better than to idealize individuation and demean connectedness — still these same feminists sometimes miss the point about Jewishness and see it only as an archaic construct to shed.

In addition, while you could say that Jews — like many other ethnics — have fuzzy boundaries, the issue of boundaries or their lack seems particularly acute for Jews. Boundaries between the self, the family, and community. Between the generations. Between history and the present. Between national identity and identification across national lines with the Jewish people. Perhaps this is why much of Jewish religion, in fact, involves drawing boundaries — between secular and sacred; between acceptable and non-acceptable food. The anguish of Israel and Palestine can be seen partly as a question of boundaries, geographical and metaphysical. Even one's body is barely one's own. A friend says, *You return from the toilet, and everyone wants to know: did you go*? The nosiness characteristic of Jewish culture relates both to responsibility and danger; if you constantly monitor information, you may be able to ward off disaster.

Fuzzy boundaries between the self, family and community can be a sign of Jewish health. And yet for Jewish women, there is danger in this lack of distinction. How do I live my life if it is not my own? There are injunctions directed at me, as a Jewish member of a larger entity, the Jewish people; as a female member of this same entity; and as a woman. They all agree on one point: *Everyone else is more important than I am*. As a Jewish woman, I need protection against these injunctions. But the therapist who attempts to point out the danger without grasping also the positive life-affirming aspect of Jewish culture forfeits my trust.

She also short-circuits my work. The immunity I develop against the "you are not important" message must be my own authentic version of self-love. This will inevitably involve sorting through the tangle of roots that nourished me,[6] separating the healthy from the diseased from the once-useful but no longer. If, as a Jew, I understand the cultural nature of much of this tangle, I come to understand myself as part of an historical process. *History is a nightmare from which I am trying to awaken*, wrote James Joyce, referring most likely to the tumultuous Ireland he was born into. But no one escapes history, however nightmarish; one can only delude oneself that one has escaped, a delusion almost identical to dominant culture consciousness in the U.S.

As an adolescent blessed with some choices, as a rebel, as a seeker of my own path I may shun the charge and privilege of historical continuity, of agency and responsibility; I may need time out. But as an adult blessed with some choices, I must wrestle my own power as, they say, Jacob wrestled the angel of god — not just to make myself happy, but to enter the historical flow. This is not a very American way to think, though it is quite Jewish.

*   *   *

Personal change, political transformation, the role of therapy: who is the self, who is the other? I know that healthy suspicion of individual solution may blur dangerously into self-hate and self-deprivation, and I have watched movements, especially feminism, exploit this blur. I also know that self-love and a sense of individual worth can slide cruelly into lack of compassion and responsibility.

This issue of therapy and politics is not particular to Jewish women, and yet Jewish women may have a particularly difficult time sorting it out. I believe that one part of healing is the struggle to change the world, to make visible and to eradicate the conditions that produced pain. I know that not every person who enters therapy is interested in changing the world, and it is a constant source of frustration to me as a teacher and writer that certain crumbs of my wisdom, such as it is, are gobbled up (*you are worthy*) while others, to me inseparable, are often ignored (*everyone else is worthy too*). I imagine that therapists experience this disappointment as well.

I also know that not every Jewish woman who seeks therapy wants to address her Jewishness; nor would I presume to dictate the form this work should take (though as a secular Jew I will also confess to disappointment that so much of it, related to or independent from therapy, has centered on religion). But since Jewishness is a collective endeavor, the work to reclaim it will be pursued with other Jewish women, in study groups, cultural activities, as well as political work as Jews. Therapists need to understand that this work can constitute in itself a healing, and that it takes courage.[7]

In January, 1989, I visited Israel and the Occupied Territories on a peace tour, and met with a variety of peace activists. One, Chaim Shur, an old-time Socialist Zionist who has worked towards Israeli-Palestinian reconciliation for most of his life, told us: *Israeli Jews are polarized, and now American Jews have to become just as polarized.*

I believe that Jewish feminists must seek and welcome this polarization. Jewish mainstream leaders, mostly male, rarely raise their voices in our behalf. They claim the right to care only about their own when people are homeless and hungry and desperate. They commemorate the Holocaust but ignore the plight of contemporary refugees. They vociferously oppose anti-Semitism but soft-pedal the horrors of racism, including Jewish racism. They exploit the energy of women, through volunteer networks and the nuclear family, without allowing us equal control of resources. Until recently they screamed for support of Israeli governmental policies, and many still actively persecute those who depart from mainstream positions.[8] Progressive American Jews, who are not represented by these leaders, must make ourselves as loud and as visible as our opposition.

This is political strategy. But it feels like splitting the family. And it feels like our fault. As daughters in Jewish homes, many of us learned to shore up the family, to protect it. Much of the work any of us do in therapy includes unlearning this protection, a counter-education that may be, as I've said, especially frightening for minorities, including Jews.

Even on the left, the people with whom we've worked closely may feel like family. Feminists, lesbians, working class people may have experienced what it means to raise charged and potentially divisive issues in a group that seemed, up until the disruption, to be getting on fine. But perhaps especially for Jews working with Jews, the familiarity may invoke childhood memory, and with it great longing and dread.

As we define our relationship to Jewishness we confront our relationship to and role in the family. For Jews who felt constrained by the growing-up demands of their family or Jewish community, who may have created some freedom through distance, the thought of engaging with any level of Jewishness will feel like rejoining the family, with all the attendant conflict. The Jewish woman with a non-Jewish partner, friends, and community, may contend not only with her own ambivalence; in addition, her non-Jewish support system may evince distaste or mystification at her new endeavor: *Why does it matter? What's so important?* She will feel alone. She will need a new support system.

Inside the Jewish community, when I criticize the Israeli government's occupation of the West Bank and Gaza, I may experience the same feelings of guilt, the same terror as a woman fighting to pray at the Western Wall in Jerusalem, or to transform the sexist language in the liturgy; the same accusations are hurled at me as at the B'nai B'rith women who recently defied the male leadership's order to dissolve their autonomous women's organization. Are we dividing the Jewish people and exposing them to danger? Are we abandoning our fathers and brothers whom we were trained to flatter and protect? Will the community of Jews reject us and will we then be alone, hated by both goyim and Jews?

Yet the truth is, Jewish women *have* disrupted the family. We have challenged patriarchal authority. We have supported affirmative action. We have created a Jewish women's peace movement in support of Israeli and Palestinian women working for peace. We have argued unequivocally for reproductive choice. We have been among the leaders of the feminist movement, challenging the traditional nuclear family. In fact, if Jewish women were to assume leadership in the Jewish community, a leadership which we are well trained to exercise, the traditionally progressive direction of a great deal of Jewish power would become even more pronounced, in support of a feminist, life-affirming agenda.

And what stops us? On the one hand, not much. The B'nai B'rith women insisting on an autonomous feminist organization have budged not one inch against the patriarchal call for "assimilation." The largely successful struggle of women rabbis for ordination, the continued battle against homophobia in the various synagogue movements, the strong pro-choice position of most mainstream Jewish groups bespeaks powerful feminist impact. Jewish women are moving, inside the Jewish community, the feminist movement, and everywhere people are fighting for liberation, dignity, peace. Name it, we're there.

But I'll ask the question again. What stops us? Sexism. Anti-Semitism. Everything I've said so far. We're afraid of division, of anger. We're constrained by our own ignorance of Jewish history and culture, by our lack of pride in who we are, our lack of trust in one another. We're reluctant to rejoin a family we gratefully escaped.

And we are afraid, deeply, irrationally afraid of our own power. How can we gather and use our power if we're afraid of what we'll do with it?

So I return to the theme of power, as I must. Isn't the point of therapy to find our power and use it, to trust what we'll do with it? Let me speak for myself. Beneath self-hate, self-distrust, something more solid and luminous reveals itself as deepest longing, for a just, generous, beautifully diverse world. My task in and out of therapy is to learn to welcome my strength, to believe that I, *I*, in all my individual and collective identities, including as a Jew, a Jewish woman, a Jewish lesbian, can help create this world—not in spite of who I am but because of it.

NOTES

1. In addition, women often find power sexy and appealing in other women, so our strength can be an asset. See Melanie Kaye/Kantrowitz, "Some Notes on Jewish Lesbian Identity," in *Nice Jewish Girls: A Lesbian Anthology*, ed., Evelyn Torton Beck (Boston: Beacon, 1989; 1st pub., 1982); e.g., "When I became a lesbian and no longer had to care what men . . . thought of me, I came into my power," p. 42.

2. See, for example, Barbara Smith, "Between a Rock and a Hard Place: Relationships Between Black and Jewish Women," in *Yours In Struggle: Three Feminist Perspectives on Anti-Semitism and Racism* (Ithaca, Longhaul Press/Fire-brand, 1984), p. 76 ff.

3. For example, Cherie Brown or the late Ricky Shereover Marcuse, whose coalition building work has been a model for the feminist anti-racist movement.

4. Proportionately more Israelis oppose in some way their government than Americans opposed ours at the peak of activity against the Viet Nam War.

5. In this it is quite distinct from Christianity, especially from Protestantism, which is the religious version of individualism.

6. The image is Bernice Mennis's, from one of our many fruitful conversations.

7. The critical importance of groups like New Jewish Agenda (a progressive multi-issue Jewish group) and Jewish Women's Call for Peace (which holds vigils in support of the Israeli Women's Peace Movement and in opposition to the occupation) is that they allow us to work *as Jews* and to use organized Jewish power in positive ways.

8. Recent studies by Steven Cohen (1989, sponsored by the Israel-Diaspora Institute at Tel Aviv University and for the American Jewish Committee) indicate that American Jews have become more dovish, and that leadership is actually more dovish than its constituent communities. On the other hand, David Biale points to retaliation in the Jewish community against leaders who advocate talking to the PLO, a Palestinian state, etc.; "The Rhetoric of Occupation," *Tikkun* (March/April 1990), 41-43.

Therapy's Double Dilemma: Anti-Semitism and Misogyny

Evelyn Torton Beck

> What public opinion should understand is that anti-semitism begins to kill with words.
>
> — Serge Klarsfeld
> *Washington Post*, May 1990

This paper begins with the premise that anti-Semitism has not been considered a serious issue in the dominant culture or in feminist communities, nor has it been adequately addressed in the therapeutic profession. The trivialization of Jewish identity issues and the widespread ignorance about Jewish history and culture have allowed anti-Semitism to combine with misogyny (and anti-Asian racism) to create the popular stereotype of the "Jewish American Princess," often referred to as the "J.A.P." This baiting of the Jewish woman must be understood as a deeply misogynist form of anti-Semitism which deflects onto the Jewish woman those negative characteristics traditionally associated with the Jewish male. This stereotyping represents a double violence, assaulting the Jewish woman both as a *woman* and as a *Jew*. The therapist who does not understand the force of this attack or the fear it engenders (espe-

Evelyn Torton Beck, PhD, is Professor and Director of Women's Studies at the University of Maryland-College Park. Among her books are *Nice Jewish Girls: A Lesbian Anthology* (1982) and *The Prism of Sex: Essays in the Sociology of Knowledge* (1979) (with Julia Sherman). She publishes and speaks widely on topics ranging from power, gender and the spectrum of difference, to feminist transformations of knowledge and feminist pedagogy.

19

cially in Jewish women) is in danger of overlooking a significant area of exploration in the therapy process.

In working with Jewish clients, it is imperative for therapists to understand that Jewish identity exists along a continuum, with religious observance (from Orthodox to Reconstruction) on one end, and secular, ethnic identification on the other (Klepfisz, 1989), with all varieties of overlapping in between. Therapists should also have a good grasp of the history of anti-Semitism and its long-term (though differential) effects upon the collective psyche of Jews and non-Jews. They must be alert to internalized anti-Semitism in their clients and in themselves if they are Jewish, and preconceptions about Jews if they are not. They must understand that Jewish clients can be deeply wounded by anti-Semitism whether they self-define as secular Jews or even as Jewish atheists. They must be sensitive to the fear and suspicion of gentiles carried by Jews, and especially the vulnerability of the Jewish woman, whose fear of being stigmatized as a "J.A.P." encourages Jewish women to split off from themselves and turn against each other. In order to maintain a positive self-image, the Jewish woman may reject the "bad" ("Jewish") component within herself, creating an identity diffusion and a sense of fragmentation. In fending off her "Jewish" self, she may externalize her bad feelings by avoiding anything Jewish and turning against her more identifiably "Jewish" sisters who possess the very characteristics from which she is trying to dissociate.

Because many people were initially unwilling to see the misogyny or anti-Semitism inherent in the construction of the term "J.A.P.," many Jewish men and women openly perpetuated the stereotype which had its beginnings in the novels of Jewish American writers (Roth, 1959; Wouk, 1955) and was further popularized by Jewish stand-up comedians. The widespread and unselfconscious use of the word "J.A.P." within Jewish communities allowed this powerfully negative image of Jews to find easy resonance within the dominant culture. But because the word "Jew" was not explicitly named in the epithet "J.A.P.," the negative association with "Jew" remained hidden even as it was perpetuated — "too Jappy" easily masked "too Jewy" — and the "J.A.P." came to embody everything that a decent person would *not* want to be.

When Jews themselves participate in creating an environment hostile to Jewish women, the dominant culture is quick to follow suit, especially in the current climate where hate crimes of all kinds are on the rise and specifically anti-Semitic incidents (some religious, some political in nature) have risen by 21 percent in the last few years. But in spite of these realities some Jews continue to insist that acts of anti-Semitism are unimportant (as compared to acts of racism), while others fear that calling attention to these acts will only result in further (possibly worse) attacks. Though such responses are neither new nor atypical, Jewish fears are rarely discussed openly (even among Jews).

In order to understand these specifically Jewish terrors, therapists need to know that there is a hidden history of anti-Semitism in the United States which manifested itself (until the end of World War Two) in open discrimination in jobs and housing, enrollment limitations in colleges, and myths of cowardice among Jewish soldiers (Belth, 1979; Gerber, 1986; Morgan, 1963; Selzer, 1972). When, after the war, the annihilation of Jews in the concentration camps was made public, open anti-Semitism became unthinkable and Jew hating went underground. Because there has never been any public education around anti-Semitism, these negative feelings have remained intact in the collective unconscious, simply waiting to be tapped (as they have been increasingly in the last decade). To the disappointment of the many Jewish women who helped organize the women's liberation movement, feminist communities have not been free of anti-Semitism either (Beck, 1982, 1984; Kaye/Kantrowitz, 1982; Miriam, 1982; Pogrebin, 1982, 1987). And in spite of how anti-Semitism marks the Jewish psyche, in the recent theoretical focus on "difference," Jewish identity remains undifferentiated from the white U.S. Christian majority and Jewish material remains absent from the emerging multi-cultural curricula of Women's Studies (Beck, 1988a; Elwell 1987). Such omissions create a vacuum in which stereotypes can flourish even in "progressive" environments.

But other factors are also at work. Resentments against the economic success of many Asian immigrants, often called "the new Jews" (*Change*, 1989), add fuel to the word "J.A.P." which harks back to popular World War Two posters that urged American citizens to fight the "yellow menace," — to "slap that Jap!" Because Japan is currently viewed as America's most serious economic competitor, these negative associations with the word "J.A.P." carry special resonances. It is no accident that in this climate of escalating class antagonism, the Jew becomes singled out as *the* symbol of upward mobility, as if the "American Dream" were not legitimate for Jews, who (as a group) have moved from working class to middle class status. Class and gender come together here, marked by the sharp increase in the number of women entering the work force, especially the professions. And it is the *Jewish* woman on whom this anger is focused in the form of jokes and public humiliation, for the Jew as "J.A.P." is blamed for the excesses of the American consumer society. Yet, there is widespread denial that the "J" in "J.A.P." has anything to do with Jews. "You do not have to be Jewish to be a 'J.A.P.'" is a common defense of the term.

Such denial makes it essential for therapists to understand that many Jews, who were brought up to view the United States as a safe haven, refuse to take anti-Semitic currents seriously even when they result in beatings of Jews as well as defacement, desecration and destruction of Jewish institutions. In the face of these realities, some Jews choose to screen out the vulnerability they feel *as Jews*. Many Jews avoid publicly identifying as Jews, though they will not actively deny it either. In varying degrees and in different ways, the Holocaust has marked the psyche of every Jew the world over. *I believe that most Jews, even the most assimilated, walk around with a subliminal fear of anti-Semitism the way most women walk around with a subliminal fear of rape.*

In such a cultural context, the escalation of the grotesque caricatures of the "J.A.P." (in books, greeting cards, cartoons, grafitti, games, T-shirts, verbal jokes, and in common speech, especially in areas where there are high concentrations of Jews) unmasks the anti-Semitism and misogyny that were already present in the more "moderate" 1950's form, when the image of the "Jewish American Princess" was enjoyed by many as a relatively "benign" figure of fun. By the end of the 1980s the image has become so venomous — the "J.A.P." as monster that needs to be annihilated — it is no longer possible to avoid reading the "J.A.P." as a substitute for the age-old stereotype of the "Jew," one which is given particular force when it is combined with (and disguised by) misogyny and fueled by anti-Asian racism.

Even a brief comparison of the characteristics attributed to the Jew and the "J.A.P." (as "Jewish American Princess") should make the parallels compelling. The traditional anti-Semitic image represents the Jew (most familiar as Shakespeare's Shylock) as manipulative, calculating, avaricious, materialistic, sexually perverse, ugly (hook-nosed), and foreign in speech. In the "Jewish American Princess" these same characteristics are combined with misogynist stereotypes associated specifically with women, to create a Jewish female who is manipulative (of men), calculating (in getting men's money), materialistic (focused only on clothing, furniture and her looks), vulgar (she sports designer clothes, furs, and conspicuous jewels) and ugly (she needs or has had a "nose job"); she is sexually both "promiscuous" and "frigid" (as the male Jew is accused of being both "communist" and "capitalist"); she is accused of trading sexuality for "goods." (Although the image of the "J.A.P." is instrinsically heterosexual, the Jewish lesbian is nonetheless not safe from being stereotyped as "J.A.P." — not even in lesbian circles.)

No aspect of the Jewish woman's body is left unmarked. The speech of the "Jewish American Princess" is presented as accented — "New York style" — in ways that recall the Jewish immigrant origins of her family (she is typically depicted shrieking loudly and crudely, "O my GAWD!"). Both the "Jew" and the "J.A.P." are represented as parasites who would suck others dry, who finally become dehumanized objects that the world would be well rid of. The litany of historical accusations against Jews here takes on a decidedly "female" cast, and the Jewish woman as "J.A.P." — a "Shylock in drag" — is made to carry the burden of the conspicuous consumption that marks U.S. society.

A series of recent incidents illustrate the parallels between the Jew and the "J.A.P." who becomes stigmatized, humiliated and finally annihilated in examples that range from harassment and psychic rape, to threats of annihilation and literal murder. On college campuses with visible Jewish populations, contests seeking the "fattest-JAP-on-campus" and T-shirts sporting "Slap-a-JAP" and

"JAP-Buster" are quite popular, especially among fraternities.* In 1986 a Cornell University booth at a campus fair featured a blown-up dummy of a fat woman with her mouth wide open, with a sign that read, "Make her prove she's not a "J.A.P.," make her swallow!" In 1988 the April Fool's issue of the Cornell *Lunatic* ran a supposedly humorous feature entitled "JAPS-B-GONE," offering a series of tips for exterminating JAPS. Also in 1988 a Boston University (Jewish male) student wrote a song (presented on the Oprah Winfrey show) entitled "The JAP Rap" which repeats as its chorus, "JAPS are the ones we must abolish." Syracuse University women were verbally assaulted when several thousand students at a game half-time stood up and, while pointing their fingers, repeatedly shouted "JAP,JAP,JAP,JAP" at women who were singled out while walking across the field; certain gathering places both in and out of doors were designated as "Jap-free zones." At The American University, dormitories heavily populated by Jewish women are mockingly known as "Tokyo Towers."

During the 1980s, "Jewish American Princess" paraphenalia became a big industry (which has since abated somewhat in response to protests by Jewish women in and outside established Jewish communities). Popular greeting cards depicted JAP-Olympics, with the Jewish woman doing "bank vaulting" instead of "pole vaulting"; or "cross-country *kvetching*" (Yiddish for whining) instead of skiing, here defined as "an irritable whine made by a three-year old child or *a JAP at any age*." The Jewish woman then, is not only represented as an all-powerful monster, but is also infantilized. She is placed in a no-win situation, for if she works in the professions (as "Bunny Bagelman" of greeting card fame), she is undermined by being made to look ridiculous, with typical "Jewish" features, wearing ostentatious jewelry inappropriate to a working woman — and always marked in some way as a Jew, sometimes with a Jewish

---

*Please note that whenever I am analyzing the term "J.A.P.," I deliberately put the word in quotes and use periods to separate the letters in order to show that each letter stands for a *real* word. Whenever I quote cartoons and other comic usages, I follow their pattern and allow the letters in JAP/Jap to run together to mirror the elision which masks the meaning of the "J." This visual difference is of particular importance to the meaning making process.

star, at other times a crown marked "JAP." One such card, made for Halloween, depicts a grotesque female figure and reads, "Is it a vampire? No, it's Bunny Bagelman with PM syndrome!" In a *Hustler* magazine continuing cartoon, "Chester the Molester" lures little Jewish girls with a trail of pennies. The intertwining of *sexism* with *anti-Semitism* becomes particularly transparent in these visual representations.

But even the rhetoric of violence in such examples does not prepare us for the most shocking incident, described by lawyer Shirley Frondorf in *The Death of a Jewish American Princess: The True Story of a Victim on Trial* (1988), in which a Jewish husband who had murdered his wife (the facts were not in dispute), successfully defended himself by depicting her as someone who had been "materialistic," who shopped and spent, nagged shrilly and bothered him at work," — in short, his wife was a "J.A.P." who, by implication, deserved what she got. That a rhetoric of violence leads to and further justifies physical violence is amply illustrated by Frondorf's work.

While Jewish feminists have repeatedly analyzed the negative impact of the "J.A.P." stereotype (Alperin, 1988; Beck, 1988b; Klagsbrun, 1987; Klein, 1980; Rubenstein, 1987; Schneider, 1984; Schnur, 1987; Siegel, 1986; Spencer, 1989) its seriousness was not acknowledged until the attacks on Jewish women led to attacks that also threatened Jewish men — when swastikas, "Kill JEWS," and "Give Hitler a second chance" graffiti appeared side by side with "Kill JAPs!" Then it became clear even to those who had previously insisted on the "harmlessness" of the stereotype that "Jap-free" zones were the equivalent of Nazi Germany's *Judenrein* ("Jew-free") spaces. Such parallels should make amply clear that assaults upon Jewish women were anti-Semitic from the start, because Jewish women are *Jews*.

In such a context, the threat of being labelled a "J.A.P." is deeply undermining to a Jewish woman's dignity, integrity, and above all, her self-esteem. The cumulative impact of these assaults on her *as a Jew* and *as a woman* is potentially devastating and allows her no place in which she feels safe. In response, some Jewish women experience shame at being Jewish, while others are eager to differentiate themselves as "good" Jews in comparison to the "J.A.P." who becomes the incarnation of the "bad" Jew. Instead of using energy to explore positive self-discovery, they focus on *not* becoming or being mistaken for the feared and hated "J.A.P." without understanding that it is being Jewish *and* female that makes them vulnerable. For young Jewish women this struggle against anti-Semitism compounds the difficulty of identity formation, since they must cope with the identity of being "other" as a Jew at the same time that they are also coping with ordinary issues appropriate to their age and stage. "You don't know what it's like to walk around in my body. It takes so much energy to defend oneself," said one young Jewish woman at a large Eastern university where "J.A.P." baiting was common. This additional expenditure of energy used to fend off potential attacks must be acknowledged and dealt with.

But therapists will not be surprised that such a powerful stereotype will also elicit defensiveness. Many young Jewish women, especially those from upper middle-class homes, deal with the cognitive dissonance set up in them by the epithet "J.A.P." by reversing its meaning (they "know" it is meant to hurt them, yet cannot bring themselves to admit it is anti-Semitic), and claiming to be proud of being a "J.A.P." When speaking on college campuses and to high school students, I have repeatedly heard young Jewish women admit that they would be offended to be called "too Jewy," but claim not to mind being called "too Jappy." Yet when confronted with this substitution these same women often experience an acute discomfort they cannot explain. They therefore insist that the people who use the term are simply envious of the material goods their parents (mainly the fathers) thrust upon them. In defending themselves (and their fathers) such women will say they are "proud" to be "princesses," proud to be the object of their fathers' affection. And perhaps the daughters' equation of love with material things is an accurate perception, given that men often are not able to show affection directly and learn to measure their own success by what they have been able to provide their families.

But such a constellation might lead therapists to wonder why the "Jewish mother" has suddenly become so invisible in the family system and to wonder what could explain her silence? It is after all the "Jewish mother" who births the "Jewish princess," yet her presence is erased in relation to her daughter. One possible perspective from which to interpret this script leads us to look more closely at the meaning of the Jewish daughter as the "little princess" who sits on Daddy's lap (even when she is grown) and then is turned into the monstrous figure of the "J.A.P." who manipulates men. Could there be some reverse projection at work here? Although Jewish families are generally not perceived as sexual environments (Klein, 1980, p.40), there is something about the family configuration embedded in the stereotype (the daughter compliant in early years, the doting father who later turns against his daughter, and the silent mother) that suggests sexual abuse or incest, or at the very least incestuous desire. Certainly we are discovering that Jewish families are not immune (as the mythology would have us believe) to any of the violence and abuse that marks other groups (Spiegel, 1987). This line of analysis raises many complex questions of vital importance to the creation of a successful therapeutic alliance. What happens to the alliance when the therapist herself holds the stereotype? Might the process of transference/counter-transference lead such a therapist to become the silent mother? How else might prejudice interfere?

But the "J.A.P." stereotype does not effect only Jewish women. It is also damaging to those Jewish men who use the stereotype — some to camouflage competitive feelings toward the Jewish women who are now entering previously all-male domains (Jewish secular and religious institutions) in large numbers. The Jewish men who "believe" in the stereotype learn to despise and mistrust Jewish women. That Jewish men's mistrust leads to a reciprocal mistrust in Jewish women is not surprising, and the resulting high rate of intermarriage must be paired with the reality of internecine gender warfare among Jews — a scenario that ultimately contributes to anti-Semitism and self-hatred (Lewin, 1948).

While the term "J.A.P." has at times been used to describe some Jewish men, the term "Jewish American Prince," never developed any bite, largely because of the double standard that admires in men the very characteristics that are considered heinous in women. Jewish men have colluded in this negative focus on the Jewish woman. In their attempt to secure a place for themselves, Jewish men have successfully deflected the anti-Semitism of the dominant culture onto the Jewish woman who is blamed *as a Jew* for participating too eagerly in the upward mobility that is the "American dream," and *as a woman* for conforming too closely to gender norms assigned to women.

Therapists must remember that stereotypes have their origins in some observable reality that is then substituted for the whole and attributed to every member of the group. Of course some Jews participate in consumerist behavior, as do members of every other group, and this value system should be critiqued wherever it occurs. But the question that needs to be kept in mind is why Jewish women are taking the rap for everyone else, including Jewish men?

While minority status creates some similarities in the issues and problems dealt with in therapy by individuals in those groups, therapists need to understand the ways in which different minorities are positioned differently in the dominant culture. *A general understanding of "outsider" status will not suffice.* What follows are a series of pragmatic suggestions that therapists can use when working with Jewish clients. These have been developed in conjunction with psychologist L. Lee Knefelkamp who works with Jewish College students across the nation:

1. Take the issue of Jewish identity and anti-Semitism seriously whether working with Jewish or non-Jewish clients.
2. Do your homework. Familiarize yourself with Jewish history and customs; study the history of anti-Semtitism and understand its cumulative effects.
3. Understand that life span developmental tasks are influenced by minority status, that Jewish women must deal with at least two sets of identity issues — those associated with life's developmental tasks and those associated with the development of Jewish identity, which the dominant Christian culture does not always support.
4. Understand how Jewish culture places inordinate pressure on women toward marriage and child-bearing and that this pressure differentially influences gender identity and sexual identity formation. Understand that pressures toward heterosexuality, marriage and child-bearing are intensified in a community

where so many millions have been exterminated in recent history.
5. Do not assume that if the therapist is either Jewish and/or feminist that s/he will have a grasp of these essential understandings necessary to working effectively with Jewish clients.

REFERENCES

Alperin, M. (1988). *Jap jokes: Hateful humor*. New York: The American Jewish Committee.

Beck, E. T. (1982). *Nice Jewish girls: A lesbian anthology*. Boston, MA: Beacon Press, revised expanded edition 1989.

Beck, E. T. (1984). Between invisibility and overvisibility: The politics of anti-Semitism in the women's movement and beyond. *Working Papers in Women's Studies*, 11, Madison, WI: Women's Studies Research Center.

Beck, E. T. (1988a). The politics of Jewish invisibility. *NWSA Journal* 1 (1), 92-102.

Beck, E. T. (1988b). From "Kike" to "J.A.P." *Sojourner: The Women's Forum*, 14 (1), 18-23.

Belth, N. C. (1979). *A promise to keep: A narrative of the American encounter with anti-Semitism*. New York: Times Books. *Change: A Magazine of Higher Learning*. (1989). Special issue on Asian and Pacific Americans (November/December).

Elwell, S. L. (1987). *The Jewish women's studies guide* (2nd ed.). Lanham, MD: University Press of America and Biblio Press.

Frondorf, S. (1988). *Death of a "Jewish American Princess": The true story of a victim on trial*. New York: Villard Books.

Gerber, D. A. (1986). *Anti-Semitism in American history*. Urbana: University of Illinois Press.

Kaye/Kantrowitz, M. (1982). Anti-Semitism, homophobia, and the Good White Knight. *off our backs: a women's newsjournal*, 12 (5), 30-31.

Klagsbrun, F. (1987). JAP: The new anti-Semitic code word. *Lilith: The Jewish Women's Magazine*, 17, 11.

Klein, J. W. (1980). *Jewish identity and self esteem*. New York: Institute on Pluralism and Group Identity, American Jewish Committee.

Klepfisz, I. (1984). Secular Jewish identity: *Yidishkayt* in America. *Tribe of Dina: A Jewish women's anthology*. Boston: Beacon Press, 32-50, revised expanded edition, 1989.

Knefelkamp, L. L. (1979). *Double identity issues of Jewish college students*. New York: B'nai Brith Publication.

Lewin, K. (1948). Self-hatred among Jews. *In* G. W. Lewins' *Resolving social conflicts*. New York: Harper & Row, 186-200.

Miriam, S. (1982). Anti-Semitism in the lesbian community. *Sinister Wisdom*, 19, 50-60.

Morgan, T. B. (1963). The fight against prejudice. *Look*, June 4, 68-77.
Pogrebin, L. (1982). Anti-Semitism in the women's movement. *Ms*, 12, 45-49, 62-75.
Pogrebin, L. (1987). Going public as a Jew. *Ms*, 16, 76-77, 194-195.
Roth, P. (1959). *Goodbye, Columbus*. New York: Houghton Mifflin.
Rubenstein, J. A. (1987). The graffiti wars. *Lilith: The Jewish Women's Magazine*, 17, 8-9.
Schneider, S. W. (1984). *Jewish and female: Choices and changes in our lives today*. New York: Simon and Schuster, pp. 27-28, 268-70, 283-86.
Schnur, S. (1987). Blazes of truth. *Lilith: The Jewish Women's Magazine*, 17, 10-11.
Selzer, M. (1972). *Kike*. New York: World Publishing Co.
Siegel, R. J. (1986). Antisemitism and sexism in stereotypes of Jewish women. *Women and Therapy: A Feminist Quarterly*, 5 (2/3), 249-257.
Spiegel, M. C. (1987) Beyond inclusion: Redefining the Jewish family. *Genesis 2: An Independent Voice for Jewish Renewal*, 18 (3), 15.
Spencer, G. (1989). An analysis of JAP-baiting humor on a college campus. *International Journal of Humor Research*, 2 (4), 329-348.
Wouk, H. (1955). *Marjorie Morningstar*. New York: Doubleday & Co.

Jewish Feminism and Women's Identity

Susannah Heschel

Jews have undergone a radical change during the last two hundred years, from religious, semi-autonomous communities living in the midst of generally hostile non-Jewish political bodies, to largely secular, areligious and assimilated citizens on equal legal footing with others. Although most American Jews today define themselves as non-religious, the traditional attitudes of classical Judaism remain strong, particularly in terms of gender roles and family structures. Those attitudes are transmitted through Jewish institutions, including synagogues, organizations such as Hadassah and Federations, as well as family traditions. Indeed, it might be argued that traditional Jewish views of women and men have persisted with greater tenacity than classical religious beliefs in God, revelation, and observance of the commandments.

Understanding contemporary Jewish women, whether secular or religious, requires awareness of the traditional Jewish teachings about women. Those teachings include Jewish laws regarding marriage and divorce, and their expression in Jewish wedding ceremonies, as well as the community's continued emphasis on heterosexual marriage; the highly circumscribed position of women in the central aspects of religious observance of Judaism, including prayer, study, and observance of the commandments; and general attitudes toward the female body and sexuality, expressed in the Bible, Talmud, and later commentaries, as well as philosophical and mystical literature.

Susannah Heschel, PhD, is an assistant professor in the Department of Religious Studies at Southern Methodist University, Dallas. She is the editor of *On Being a Jewish Feminist: A Reader*, as well as numerous articles on feminist theology, and is the author of a forthcoming study entitled, *The Quest of the Jewish Jesus: Christian and Jewish Versions*.

Traditional teachings have an impact on the sense of self, as well as familial and communal attitudes, even when Jews assert their rejection of religion in favor of a secular identity. Therapists working with Jewish women should be aware of the traditional attitudes toward Jewish women in order to better understand the roots of problems, particularly self-esteem, and to assist women in their self-understanding.

Judaism as a religion and historical experience has been shaped almost exclusively by men, as attested by the standard Jewish history textbooks which almost never mention women (Seltzer, 1980). Although, increasingly, studies of aspects of Jewish women's history are being undertaken, women-authored sources remain limited to the modern period; the earliest extant writing by a Jewish woman is a 17th century European autobiography (Lowenthal, 1977). The experience of women within Judaism must therefore be described and evaluated on the basis of what has been written about them by men. Inevitably, such writings must be interpreted with care, since they reflect male attitudes toward women, rather than women's own self-understanding. Representations of women in male texts often refer to an abstract "female," whose purpose is to serve as a foil against which maleness may be defined, rather than to the femaleness experienced by women. Nonetheless, patterns emerge over the course of Jewish history that define femaleness with some degree of ambivalence; there is, for example, both a feminine aspect of divinity (Shekhinah) and a female demon (Lilith). Those patterns may be traced both in what is stated concerning women in Jewish texts, and in what is unstated.

The female and male roles regulating the lives of Jewish women and men are set forth in the system of commandments described in the Bible and the Talmud (Biale, 1985). Both the Bible and Talmud were believed to contain the words of the revelation of God to the Israelites at Mt. Sinai; as God's word they are believed eternal, immutable, and absolutely binding. Talmudic law itself was further explicated by subsequent generations of male rabbis who clarified, elaborated, and only rarely modified or eliminated the regulations. In addition to laws, the Talmud and its commentaries (known as rabbinic literature) contain informal teachings, moral exhortations, legends, biblical interpretations, and various kinds of advice, ranging from spiritual to medicinal.

In the modern period major changes have occurred in the status of Jewish religious belief and practice. Beginning in the eighteenth century Jews in Western and Central Europe gradually were able to achieve political and social emancipation from the restrictive regulations of the various European principalities where they lived (Katz, 1973). This meant a freedom to practice Judaism in any way they chose, or to live a secular life without concern for religion.

Judaism itself was modernized, and alternatives to Orthodoxy emerged, including Reform, Conservative, and Reconstructionist Judaism, as well as secular movements of Jewish socialism and Zionism. These movements dislodged the traditional position of both the rabbi and the Talmud as the central authorities for the Jewish community. Yet even as traditional beliefs concerning God and revelation were abandoned and the adherence to the commandments waned, traditional role distinctions and definitions of femaleness were not eliminated, but simply given new expression. For example, in Orthodox synagogues women sit apart from men, generally separated by a curtain, balcony, or decorative fence. In most non-Orthodox synagogues women and men sit next to each other. Sex role definitions are regulated by the activities relegated to women and men within the synagogue: women may be generally expected to serve food and drink at the reception following the service, whereas men may be expected to function as ushers; at Friday evening services, women may say blessings over candles, men over wine.

The role differentiation between women and men is not without clear value assignment in traditional Judaism. Simone de Beauvoir's categories of man as "subject" and woman as "other" are confirmed when applied to Judaism (de Beauvoir, 1953). Women's otherness is defined in Jewish law, which regulates nearly every aspect of men's lives; women are discussed when they impinge upon a man's life, such as marriage and divorce. Women are exempt from certain categories of ritual commandments, particularly those involving public activities. Frequently those commandments that pertain exclusively to women simply reinforce woman as other, since they are performed not for the woman herself, but for the sake of a man. For example, the body of regulations concerning women's ritual impurity require women to immerse in a special ritual bath following menstruation, childbirth, and any discharge.

Prior to the immersion, during the period of "impurity," women do not suspend any of their religious or social obligations; they continue to observe commandments and are not barred from the synagogue. The only restriction is contact with a man, because he is said to contract impurity from contact with an "impure" woman. In actual practice, the regulation means that marital relations are suspended for about two weeks each month (the impurity is defined as the menstrual period followed by seven days without any discharge). Immersion in the ritual bath, then, is not for the sake of the woman — to return her to the community or to enhance her spiritual life — but for the sake of her husband. He is the actual subject of the commandment, for whose sake the woman, as other, carries it out.

Woman's otherness is also encoded in Jewish divorce laws. Although the non-Orthodox denominations have liberalized the rules somewhat, classical Jewish law stipulates that a man divorces his wife; a woman may not divorce her husband, but simply request that he divorce her. In another example, nearly all visual images of Jews, particularly religious Jews, are of male Jews. The holy, pious Jew is nearly always portrayed as an elderly man with a long, white beard. The equation of Jewishness with maleness is supported not only by women's exclusion from those traditional religious practices central to Judaism — prayer and study — but by the absence of positive images of women as holy. Frequently, femininity is used in classical Jewish sources, including the Bible, as a metaphor for immorality. In Isaiah 3, for example, a long passage describes the immoral behavior of the daughters of Zion with a long recitation of various items associated with femininity: bracelets, trinkets, cloaks, veils, and so forth. The conclusion of the passage warns that God will "lay bare [their] secret places," a verse suggesting that as punishment the women will either be raped or rendered infertile by God. Further dissociations of women with holiness in classical Judaism are reinforced by efforts to hide women's bodies from public view, based on the fear of their alleged seduction of men. The requirements of modest dress for women varied in stringency during the course of Jewish history; the most stringent came with Hasidism, a pietistic movement that arose during the eighteenth century in Eastern Europe and continues, in diminished numbers, today. Hasidic women are expected to cover their legs, arms, chests, backs, necks, and, once married, their hair. Hasidic synagogues tend to have the greatest possible separation of women from men's view. Nonetheless, the Hasidic movement saw the publication of numerous pamphlets to advise men about eliminating distracting, sexual thoughts that entered their minds during prayer. The absence of women, in other words, does not guarantee the intended goal.

Woman as sexual temptress was extended to a demonization of the female in the mythical figure of Lilith, who first appears in rabbinic and medieval biblical commentaries, as well as folkloric sources, and who continued to be active in the Jewish popular imagination throughout the centuries (Cantor, 1983). According to traditional commentaries, Lilith was the first woman created by God, along with Adam, but she was expelled from the Garden of Eden after refusing to obey Adam's commands. God replaced her with Eve. As punishment for her disobedience to Adam, Lilith, according to the legends, is forced to give birth to one hundred babies each day, and also witness the death of one hundred of her children each day. Her punishment is thus both the physical pain of childbirth and the emotional pain of loss of children. In the popular imagination, Lilith came to represent a demonic figure who might kill innocent babies who are unprotected, harm women during childbirth, or seduce men into sinful nocturnal emissions. Various amulets were developed to protect against Lilith's power, and these attest to the strength attributed to her in the popular imagination. The female was not held to be powerless in Jewish tradition, but her power was named evil, rather than holy.

At the other end of the spectrum from Lilith, however, medieval Jewish mysticism developed as a central tenet belief in a female aspect of God. According to the mystical tradition, God's holy presence, the Shekhinah, is feminine and dwells as an immanent divine presence in the world, having gone into exile with the Jewish people. Redemption is defined as both a divine and a human need, divine redemption defined as the reunion of the feminine with the masculine aspect of God. In other Jewish spiritual writings, the community of Israel is hypostasized as female, and generally presented as the bride of God. Similarly, the Sabbath is described as a queen, for whom the home and family must be prepared with a welcome. That God and the Jewish people might be described as female did not, however, bring about any recorded changes in the status of women within the Jewish community. In addition, the individual authors of Jewish mystical texts were all men, and women were excluded from sanctioned study of the doctrines.

Women's spirituality during the course of Jewish history remains a relatively unexplored topic. The research that has been conducted indicates that special prayers and biblical commentaries composed, primarily by men, for women's use reinforced negative attitudes toward sexuality. Praise for women arises in traditional Judaism primarily in relation to housekeeping functions. The biblical book of Proverbs, chapter 31, describes the "woman of virtue" as one who sews, cooks, cleans, and manages the household. She is praised, in other words, for her actions on behalf of others, rather than for intrinsic virtues. She is needed by her family and extended household, but not by the Jewish religious community, which, until recent reforms accepted by most congregations of Conservative, Reform, and Reconstructionist Judaism, excludes her from the quorum of ten required for communal prayer, from rabbinical ordination, from serving as a witness in a Jewish court of law, from study of Talmud, from divorcing her husband, and from other communal functions.

Women's exclusion from communal religious affairs — which has been drastically altered during the past twenty years by the non-Orthodox communities — is based on an unstated assumption that the Jewish community consists exclusively of men. For example, women are not to be called to the Torah to recite a blessing during Sabbath synagogue services, according to the Talmud, "for the sake of the honor of the congregation." The clear assumption is that it is men's honor, not women's, that is at stake. Similarly, a prayer on Sabbath mornings asks for God's blessing on "this congregation, its wives, sons, and daughters," again equating the congregation with men. Even the language of biblical commandments demonstrates an implied audience of men, inasmuch as the "you" to whom the commandments are addressed is gendered as male in the Hebrew text. That point is underscored by Exodus 19, when God, just prior to the revelation at Mt. Sinai, tells Moses to inform the Children of Israel to prepare themselves for the revelation by washing their clothes and sanctifying themselves. Moses then tells the

Israelites to "be ready for the third day [of revelation]; do not go near a woman." While later traditional Jewish commentaries claim that women were definitely present in the audience for the Sinai revelation, the command of Moses is obviously directed exclusively at men, and carries the implication, once again, that women are to be avoided prior to a religious experience.

The religious experience of Judaism was secularized during the modern period, with the vast majority of Jews rejecting the authority and relevance of the traditional commandments. Within the modern secular movements that define Jewish identity, however, significant new motifs regarding women emerge. In the rejection of traditional Jewish piety, Zionist writers who called for the establishment of a state of Israel claimed that the Jewish history of the past two thousand years had to be "overcome." The Hebrew meaning of "overcome" is, literally, "to become a man" (Glazer,1981). Zionism developed the idea of the new Jew, who replaced study and prayer with the sword and development of the land. The emphasis on traditional masculine imagery in Zionist writing has led feminist critics to point out the exclusion of the female and women.

That Judaism, in its religious forms, is emasculating was suggested by the Jewish philosopher Spinoza (17th century). With the development of the phenomenon of Jewish self-hatred, which took literary expression in Central Europe at the beginning of the twentieth century, Judaism was accused of being a "feminine" religion. Other Jews argued the contrary, that Judaism's commandments make it a masculine religion, in contrast to the spiritual romanticism of Christianity.

The modern representations of Judaism as feminine or masculine have also developed contradictory images of women. In popular folklore today there are contradictory stereotypes of the Jewish mother and the so-called Jewish American Princess. The former is entirely self-sacrificing on behalf of her family, while the latter is entirely selfish and exploitative of her family. With the breakdown of previous structures that provided social coherence for Jews in the pre-modern period, including the synagogue, rabbinical leadership, and communal autonomy, contemporary emphasis has been placed on the family as the central focus of Jewish life (Carlebach, 1981). The development of family rhetoric, with claims that Judaism demands a traditional housekeeping role for women, was combined with evocations of the Holocaust to warn that the Jewish population must be increased. The appearance of the rhetoric was simultaneous with the rise of the feminist movement (Baum, Hyman & Michel, 1976). In response, Gay and Lesbian synagogues have been established in several United States cities (Balka & Rose, 1990). Most Jewish communal functions remain, however, a "Noah's Ark," to which attendance is generally expected in heterosexual couples (Kaplan, 1983).

During the past twenty years, Jewish feminism has made an important impact on the Jewish community. Women are now ordained rabbis in the Conservative, Reconstructionist, and Reform movements; women are usually granted equality with men in performing synagogue rituals; women are now able to study traditional religious texts and earn doctorates in Judaic Studies. At the same time, certain problems remain. The Reconstructionist Rabbinical College ordains Gay and Lesbian rabbis, but prejudice against them within the Jewish community makes employment difficult. The language of the official prayerbooks of the denominations remains exclusively male, with God described as Father, King, and so forth, despite disclaimers that "God is neither male nor female; he is above gender." While some recognition is now given by Jewish social service agencies to problems of wife abuse, such issues remain treated, for the most part with embarassment rather than condemnation. Whereas the Roman Catholic Bishops of the United States issued a statement condemning sexism as a sin, nothing comparable has emerged from any Jewish organization (Anonymous, 1988).

The implications for Jewish women are ambiguous. Many deny the existence of sexism within Judaism, claiming instead that women are honored and powerful within the community. When a role is believed to be ordained by God, to whom one must submit willingly and with joy, it becomes even more difficult to question it. Often, there is a desire not to examine further, to avoid confronting the sexism that might be uncovered. Some of that reluctance may stem from awareness that little change can be expected. Feminists who do examine Judaism's sexism often question whether remaining a Jew is desirable. Yet feminism has also created the possibility for women to identify as Jews by encouraging new options.

With the Jewish feminist movement there have developed groups of women throughout the Jewish world who meet for prayer, discussion, and creative ritual, and who also agitate for change within the larger Jewish community. For Jewish women who do not see themselves reflected in the images and roles set forth by classical Judaism, the task is to develop an identity that will combine the values of feminism with those of Judaism. Feminist therapists can be crucial in making women aware that the negative stereotypes regarding femaleness they have internalized are derived from classical male-authored Jewish texts. A more positive appreciation of Jewish identity can be fostered by encouraging women to reject Judaism's sexism. Therapists should point out that women must not simply accept inherited traditions, but must define their own sense of what it means to be Jewish and female.

REFERENCES

Anonymous. (1988). *Partners in the mystery of redemption: A pastoral response to women's concerns for church and society*, First Draft. Washington, D.C.: National Conference of Catholic Bishops.

Balka, C., & Rose, A. (1990). *Twice blessed: On being lesbian, gay and Jewish*. Boston: Beacon Press.

Baum, C., Hyman, P., & Michel, S. (1976). *The Jewish woman in America*. New York: Dial Press.

Biale, R. (1985). *Jewish women in Jewish law*. New York: Schocken Books.

Cantor, A. (1983). The Lilith question. In S. Heschel (Ed.), *On being a Jewish feminist: A reader* (40-50). New York: Schocken Books.

Carlebach, J. (1981). Family structure and the position of Jewish women. In W. Mosse, A. Pauker, & R. Rürup (Eds.), *Revolution and evolution: 1848 in German-Jewish history*. Tübingen: J. C. B. Mohr.

De Beauvoir, S. (1953). *The second sex*, trans. H. M. Parshley. New York: Knopf.

Glazer, M. (1981). *Burning air and a clear mind*. Athens, OH: Ohio University Press.

Kaplan, R. F. (1983). The Noah syndrome. In S. Heschel (Ed.), *On being a Jewish feminist: A reader* (167-170). New York: Schocken Books.

Katz, J. (1973). *Out of the ghetto: The social background of Jewish emancipation, 1770-1870*. New York: Schocken Books.

Lowenthal, M. (Ed.) (1977). *The memoirs of Glückel of Hameln*. New York: Schocken Books.

Seltzer, R. (1980). *Jewish people, Jewish thought*. New York: Macmillan Company.

How Is This Feminist Different from All Other Feminists? Or, My Journey from Pirke Avot to Feminist Therapy Ethics

Laura S. Brown

Whenever I review the writing that has emerged from my work as a feminist therapist, one of the most resilient themes is that of the relationship of my Jewishness to my feminism. Time and again I find myself quoting Jewish law and interpretation to explain the point of feminist therapy theory that I am making, or using metaphors that find their origins in Jewish experience to throw light on life in lesbian feminist communities. While I belong to many different groups—woman, lesbian, disabled, baby boomer, psychologist, upper middle class, lover of rain and trashy novels—my primary sense of myself is as a Jew. It is my first identity, the core around which all else has been built and shaped. Consequently, my feminist identity is inextricably linked to that Jewishness.

But this connection is not an intuitively obvious one. Judaism, like all religions, is patriarchal, sexist, not implicitly supportive of a

Laura S. Brown, PhD, is a clinical psychologist in the private practice of feminist therapy in Seattle, WA. In her past life she was a campus Jewish activist and Hebrew school teacher. This article is written in loving memory of those who inspired it: my Hebrew school teachers Leah Levin, Mrs. Tischkoff, and Si Levine, and my maternal grandmother, Pauline Landau Schwartzberg.

Author's note: A glossary of the Hebrew and Yiddish terms used here will be found at the end of the article. The title of this article refers to the opening lines of the Four Questions asked by the youngest child at the Passover Seder to initiate the telling of the story of redemption from Egypt; the questions begin, "Mah nishtanah," "How is this different?"

feminist or egalitarian agenda. The Jewish cultural experiences out of which I and my family emerged did not contain any explicit expressions of a feminist politic. Lesbians were among those phenomena only to be found among non-Jews. So how did being a Jew make me into a feminist, and more specifically, into a lesbian feminist therapist very interested in ethics in therapy as practiced in lesbian communities? This article traces what I believe to be the path of that connection, a path which in many ways is idiosyncratic to my experiences as a Jew in my time, my country, and my setting, and in other ways parallels that of all the millions of Jews whose culture and religion set them on the path of progressive politics since the Haskalah (Enlightenment) of the early 1800's.

B'reyshit..in the beginning, I am the oldest grandchild of four people who came to the U.S. in the early 1900's from the Pale of Settlement in Russian-occupied Poland. My mother's parents, especially her mother, were fiercely secular Zionists; my grandma railed until her death against "Frummers," religious Jews, because her father, a Hassid, had given the money she earned running the family business to his Rebbe. My father's parents were Workman's Circle socialists who sent him to Yiddish schools, and who had drifted back to observance in the Conservative Jewish movement; my Bobe was the keeper of Yiddishkeit, the one who made sure we learned to love traditional food and celebrate the holidays. With all four grandparents alive, we had to divide up the names; the Schwartzbergs were Grandma and Grandpa, the Browns, with their assimilated new last name, Bobe and Zeyde. In my family, we started learning to live with contradictions before we knew what the word was. Both of my parents are college educated; both experienced anti-Semitism in all of its forms growing up in the working-class Jewish neighborhoods of Cleveland, and attending private colleges that had exclusionary quotas for Jews in the 1940's. I was born into a strong Jewish identity that was many-faceted.

Some of my earliest memories are of Chanukah parties at which the whole extended Brown family gathered and I, as the eldest of my generation, got made much over by older second cousins and numerous aunts and uncles. But I really began to learn what Jewish meant when my parents moved into the middle class, and into a previously all-Christian neighborhood. I didn't know yet that I "looked Jewish"; all I knew at the age of five was that the big girls from around the block had told me that I couldn't ride my bike there because I was a Jew. When I weepingly brought this news home to my parents, they explained to me that yes, I was Jewish, and that was something to be proud of. They told me then that one thing Jews believed in was in not treating people badly because of who they were. The big girls were wrong to treat me badly, but this was nothing new for Jews. The beginning of my Jewish identity is thus linked to the beginning of a progressive politic and an awareness of oppression. I was a Jew (whatever that meant) and I didn't treat people badly who were different from me. But some people were mean to those who were different; that had happened before, and it was wrong then and now.

It may have been that episode that led my parents to join a schul and send me quickly to its Sunday morning kindergarten classes, where I learned some more about this Jewish business. This was the next lesson I got about being a Jew; if you're going to be hassled about being different, know who you are and where you come from. Pride in your heritage and knowledge of your culture were the best defenses against anti-Semitism. More lessons followed when it became apparent that the other kids in my upper-middle class public school celebrated something called Christmas on the day after my birthday, and had beautiful trees in their homes, for which I begged to no avail. "Don't be a sheep wanting to follow the flock," said my parents; this was translated by my young mind into the notion that Jews, who did not celebrate this Christmas thing, didn't mind-lessly go along with the crowd no matter how pretty the decorations were on those trees.

In second grade I started afternoon Hebrew school. At my syna-gogue, girls usually didn't take that route; Bat Mitzvah was op-tional, and thus so was Hebrew school for girls, since the point of these after-school classes, in contrast to the Sunday and Sabbath school courses attended by everyone, was to prepare children for Bar and Bat Mitzvah. In a class of twenty or twenty-five kids, I was always one of three or four girls. My grandma had given an un-knowingly feminist message to her two daughters to be educated, prepared, capable of doing whatever men could. My mother passed it along to me; of course I would go to Hebrew school no matter what my gender. My parents wanted me to be a Jewishly well-educated person.

Congregation Beth Am's afternoon Hebrew school was probably like many in the American suburbs in the early 1960's. Most of the kids didn't want to be there, and were suffering through the time until Bar Mitzvah and liberation from Jewish education. The teachers were a varied bunch; most of them were pious men and women with no formal education in Jewish pedagogy who taught full time in the public schools, then spent the rest of the afternoon trying to ride herd on us. They spoke old-fashioned Ashkenazic Hebrew, with its soft sounds and slurred vowels; there was little by way of formal curriculum. We learned by learning to read Torah and commentaries. We learned the Aleph-Bes not in alphabetical order, but as it emerged in the saying, "Torah tsivah lanu Mosheh" (The Law, given to us by Moses). Hebrew and Jewishness were integrated one into the other and learned simultaneously.

So I was introduced to Jewish religious thought early. And I was lucky in my teachers, because I had some who were as interested in getting us to understand what we were reading as they were in having us daven (pray out loud) as fast as possible. Since I was good at the understanding part, and not so hot at speed-davening, I especially enjoyed the time we took for discussion.

Si Levine was my favorite teacher; he had been my father's Bar Mitzvah coach, and I think he had a soft spot in his heart for this second generation of Browns he was teaching. In his class, when I was a public school fifth grader, we studied Vayikra, the book of Leviticus. Several concepts burned themselves into my memory and my identity in Si's classroom. The first came from a scene where the Law is being presented to the Jewish people assembled at Sinai and God says, "I therefore put before you this day good and evil, death and life. Therefore, choose life." Si stopped the reading and led us in discussion. Jews, he pointed out, did not mindlessly follow, nor did God expect us to. (Ah-hah, I thought, here's where this sheep not following the flock business came from.) God expected us to make choices, and this was part of how we, as Jews, were different from others. This discussion was shortly followed by the reading of Parshat K'doshim, the section of Torah that begins with the words, "And God said to Moses, Speak to the Children of

Israel and say to them, you shall be holy (kadosh) because I your God am holy." (NB; I can remember this so clearly that as I write this in an airplane on the way to visit Bobe in Miami Beach, the line emerges from the brain cells with no reference to a printed page.)

Si stopped us there for another discussion. What was all this Kadosh stuff about? Well, Parshat K'doshim goes into some detail about this with dietary laws, sexual restrictions, and rules about the impurity of menstrual blood and semen, but Si wasn't interested in all that (besides, he knew better than to say "menstrual" or "semen" in front of a group of preadolescent suburban kids). He wanted us to think about the shoresh, the root of the word Kadosh; one of the important parts of learning Hebrew grammar and syntax is to know the root of the word so that it can be properly placed and given meaning. Kadosh meant "set apart, different from," said Si; Jews were set apart; we were different and that was good, that was holy. In the conformist days of the early 1960's this was amazingly radical, although it took me a while to know that it was. More importantly, into my growing Jewish identity went the value of being different, and the okayness of being apart and of making choices that were not the same as everyone else's as long as you chose life.

Next year, we were with Mrs. Tischkoff and studied Pirke Avot, the Sayings of the Sages. Mrs. T. was not my most favorite Hebrew teacher (she gave more points for fast davening than for good translation, and I hated not to be first), but she, like Si, was concerned that we learn the meaning of what we read and be Jews in mind as well as tongue. Pirke Avot is a collection of pithy aphorisms spoken by the groups of sages who over time compiled the Talmud. I suppose the powers-that-be thought it would be a good idea to give kids some easily recalled directives before they had their Bar or Bat Mitzvah and quit Hebrew school. The saying that has stuck with me forever, and which I've quoted often in my writing on ethics in feminist therapy, was a saying from Hillel, "Al tiphrosh meen hatzibur"; don't separate yourself from your community.

Again, we stopped for discussion. Mrs. Tischkoff asked us to think about the people who wrote Pirke Avot. They were rabbis and scholars, but they were also, as we knew, carpenters and ditchdiggers and shoemakers. In other words, she said, these folks had to help their neighbors, their communities, interpret and live with The Law in times and places where its direction and application were not always clear. If they were to make law for their communities, they had to remain a part of them, not aloof from them.

So now I had some more stuff to go into the "what does it mean to be a Jew" definition. Jews were fair and didn't discriminate; Jews had minds of their own, didn't follow flocks, and made choices. Jews were different and that was okay. And the leaders and teachers of a community were never to be separate from it. Unconsciously, I was also learning something else about being a Jew; we interpreted things. No line of Torah was left unanalyzed. From early exegesis does the tendency to thinking like a therapist grow!

In seventh grade, I began to attend pre-Bat Mitzvah class with Leah Levin. Of all the girls born in 1952, less than ten of us in my schul were Banot Mitzvah; our small class was an elite gathering in which Mrs. Levin could introduce us to Haftorah trup (the musical notation of Jewish liturgy, which differs depending on whether Torah or Haftorah is being read, and also varies between High Holiday and standard trups). Too, she taught us about the special ritual obligations of Jewish womanhood; in an all-girl class it was relatively safe to talk about menstruation and the mikvah. A lover of the language, she introduced us to the literal and figurative poetry of Hebrew.

Mrs. Levin valued adolescent girls, and women's experiences. I did not know until finding feminism how rare that was. She introduced me to the women poets of the Second Aliyah; she loved the fact that I loved to learn, and could sing well and picked up trup quickly and easily. She encouraged me to continue my Jewish education past Bat Mitzvah; she modeled for me a Jewishly educated, Jewishly knowledgeable woman. It was she, too, who had the unfortunate task of explaining to me why, as a female person, I was barred from leading services, from being the Baal Koreh, the "Master of Reading." She introduced me to the reality of sexism in Jewish life, although she did not have the word; she simply told me that it was not fair, and validated my outrage when I was denied the rewards of other star Hebrew students in leading our student congregation and being called to the Torah. In 1965, the year I had my Bat Mitzvah, women rabbis were not even a glint on the horizon, but Mrs. Levin taught me to want full privileges as a powerful person even as she trained me in the practices of the separate but not equal ritual life of an observant Jewish woman. Leah Levin continued the process started by my grandma of weaving together Jewishness and feminism. She gave me a copy of the books of the prophets in Hebrew as a Bat Mitzvah gift, inscribed in her fine Hebrew script to her "talmidah metzuyenet," her excellent student. She sent me into Jewish adulthood with words of social justice that I would grow to live by.

So when I encountered the Women's Movement in 1971, it made perfect sense to me, whose primary identity was still as a Jew (I was then the campus coordinator for the Radical Zionist Alliance and a gadfly at Hillel). Feminism spoke to me more loudly than did the Jewish community at that point, but it spoke a familiar voice. Don't discriminate; don't be a sheep; being different is okay. Make choices, and be sure they are informed ones. Cry out against injustice; never accept persecution as a norm. Act in ways that are empowering of others, while caring of self. Have an identity that is relational, a part of a community.

At that particular moment, though, I had no idea that being a Jew and a Feminist had anything in common, since the sense of familiarity was felt rather than reasoned. One of the first places to which I applied my new feminist analysis was to the Jewish community I had known, and the sexist laws and traditions of which I had been a target. I would often say to women that my first experience of overt gender discrimination had happened in Hebrew school. I was angrier at the Jewish community for having been sexist because I somehow felt that it made no sense in the context of all I had learned about justice being a core Jewish virtue. I changed my focus from Jewish to feminist activism, and began to drift away from the Jewish community, whose sexism was so clear to me because I had known it so intimately.

At first, it made perfect sense to me that I no longer attended services, celebrated holidays, or hung out mainly with other Jews; instead I was going to women's events and spending time with lesbians and feminists. But slowly and over the last almost two decades, the connections between my Jewish roots and my feminist identity have been redrawn to the point where they are woven together so tightly that I am amazed at how they ever fell apart. The first "click" came when reading an article about the relationship of the lesbian community to lesbian separatism. The author, also a Jewish lesbian, used the analogy of the relationship between assimilated and observant Jews. The latter would always make the former uncomfortable, she pointed out, because they reminded the assimilated that they were truly the "other," not a part of the mainstream, there only on sufferance for as long as the group in power allowed them to be. Separatists, "obvious" lesbians, fulfilled the same function for those of us who passed or assimilated into patriarchy to greater or lesser degrees. I nodded, read on, thought again and some more, realizing that there were many parallels between the lives of Jews in the Diaspora, and the lives of lesbians and women in patriarchy. I also realized that this was an analogy that could only completely make sense if you had been raised in an assimilated Jewish community and had heard the anger and ambivalence about "obvious" Jews that I had always heard, or had struggled, as I had, to both fit in and hold onto your identity when you declined for the umpteenth time to sing Christmas carols at the school concert.

My realization of the uniqueness and importance of my Jewish experiences also grew out of the context of my life as a lesbian feminist who happened to be Jewish in places where there were no Jews. I was finding it harder and harder to sustain a primary connection to what was essentially a non-Jewish community; having moved to attend graduate school in a small town in southern Illinois where Jews were a scarce commodity, I found myself missing familiar (i.e., Jewish) rhythms of life when I tried to become a part of an entirely non-Jewish women's community. Lesbians in Carbondale mostly played softball or drank beer; I, raised in a Jewish tradition that down-played the importance of sports, and emphasized the importance of not getting drunk except on Purim, didn't quite fit in. To my surprise, I felt more at home as a feminist with a sister graduate student, Nechama Liss-Levinson. I had expected to be put off by an Orthodox Jewish married woman; after all, the traditions that she upheld in her life represented what I was critical of in Judaism. But Nechama's feminism felt familiar; it felt Jewish. Our ideas of how to put our politics into action were similar; when in doubt, start a psychology of women class so that women would know who we were and where we came from.

After that initial experience of reconnection, I began increasingly to ask myself if I could find the roots of the philosophies that informed my assumptions and my judgements as a lesbian-feminist. It began to be apparent that the core of my thinking, and the criteria against which I measured new ideas, were the set of norms about being a Jew in the world that I had absorbed first in my family and then in Hebrew school every afternoon. I decided that I wanted to stop passing, to proudly and overtly claim my Jewishness as the source of my thinking. But this meant coming to terms with contradictions. As have many feminist Jews and Jewish feminists, I struggled to come up with a Midrash, an interpretation, I could live with. How could I take what worked from Judaism without accepting the rest; the laws proclaiming menstrual blood unclean, the laws calling same-sex love an abomination, the xenophobia and national chauvinism of the growing right wing of Zionism?

In order to do this, I went back to what I had learned to be the core of Jewish thought in the first place. "Two Jews, three schuls," my grandmother had told me; to be a Jew is to live with contradictions and diversity. While I might not follow Halacha, I could still own the importance of a particular way of understanding good and evil, relationships between people, the nature of community. Thus, it honors my Jewish core to allow the contradictions to live within me. "Choose life," says Torah; "Don't separate yourself from your community," admonishes Hillel. And another refrain; "Pikuach nefesh," the saving of a life, is so important that you may break almost any other law, even the laws of Kashrut and Shabbat, in order to fulfill this highest law. Feminism is, to me, about the saving of women's lives; if being a lesbian feminist therapist meant that I was not living halachically, I was fulfilling what I saw as more basic injunctions for a Jew.

I was also learning about the subtle ways in which self-hatred is internalized and expressed. I realized that my expectations for Judaism, for Jews, as for feminism and women, were unrealistically purist. I was requiring *this* religion, *this* cultural tradition, to be freer of sexism and homophobia than any other before I would find it acceptable, just as I (and other feminists) expected women to be more caring, loving, giving, and tolerant. I had been less forgiving of that which I could neither accept nor agree with in Jewishness than I was of traditions to which I had no connection. What I learned as a therapist is that the expectation of perfection is a defense against shame, and that this expectation embodies the notion that the "other," be it Jew or woman, is evil unless sinless. In confronting this aspect of my self-hatred as a Jew, and allowing my heritage to be what it was, a mixed bag, I could also come to think more clearly as a feminist about this other oppressed community in which I had come to live, and to see and confront that community's anti-Semitism.

This re-visioning of Jewish ethics through the lens of feminist thought has been a powerful factor in helping me to understand my processes of developing feminist therapy theory and practice, especially in the area of ethical dilemmas. The parallels between the lives of Jews and the work of the "avot" (the sages of the Talmud) and the lives of lesbian and feminist therapists in our communities have continued to amaze and inform me. The questions dealt with by Jews historically—passing and assimilation versus identity and integrity; living with ethics and norms that vary from those of the larger community; dealing creatively with the ever-present threat of violence in our lives without becoming damaged or diminished by that threat; creatively addressing our diversity and empowering each other to greater autonomy in the world while preserving our precious connections to one another—all of these are concerns that are feminist, and all are questions addressed in my Jewish education because they were central to the lives and survival of Jews. I can celebrate how immeasurably I am enriched by having access to two thousand years of strategies and solutions for survival; I can also see how the development of diverse and sometimes hostile streams of thought within the Jewish community has contributed to that survival, and to our continued ability to thrive with our intact Jewish identities in the face of both genocide and the seduction of assimilation. This is what I want for the community of women. My feminist self borrows freely from the experience and collective unconscious of my Jewish self.

This integration of Yiddishkeit and feminist thought has shaped an approach that guides my own questions about feminist therapy theory, especially in the development of standards for practice among feminist therapists. I have come to use Jewish experience and ethics as a template for my feminist theorizing. When addressing a question of ethics in feminist therapy, I first ask myself how I might understand the matter at hand Jewishly. I look to Jewish ethical writings, folklore and traditions to ask how Jews have dealt with problems of living that now face lesbians and feminists. I examine the lives of Jewish scholars and teachers for clues about how lesbian and feminist therapists living and working among our communities can lead our lives in ways that respect our boundaries and our needs for nurturance as well as those of our clients. I engage in "pilpul," the dialectical arguments that Talmudic scholars have pursued over the ages in which divergent truths are explored and analyzed in order to achieve clarity.

In the midst of writing this article, I had a long conversation about the meaning of Jewishness with my youngest brother. He is a "Baal T'shuvah," a Jew who has returned to strict observance after falling away from Jewishness. His construction of Jewishness is perforce stricter than mine. Yet when I told him about writing this piece, and about my definitions of what it meant to be living Jewishly in the world, he agreed with me. I was not too surprised. Two Jews, different "schuls," but in agreement that choice, empowerment, community, justice, and the willingness to go the distance to save a life are all basic to thinking like a Jew. To rephrase the famous words of Hillel to the non-Jew who wished to be taught all of the Law while standing on one foot, "Don't oppress others in ways you wish not to be oppressed. All the rest is commentary." My feminist commentary stands within that tradition; Jewish thinker and feminist therapist are inextricably interwoven in me.

A GLOSSARY OF HEBREW AND YIDDISH TERMS

N.B.: These definitions reflect my understanding of their meaning. H. = Hebrew, Y. = Yiddish

Aleph-Bes (H. and Y.) — Literally, the first two letters of the Hebrew alphabet in their Ashkenazi pronounciation; the ABC's.

Ashkenazi (H.) — Literally "German," an adjective referring to Jews from Europe. Ashkenazic Hebrew pronounciation is different from that used in Israel, where Sephardic (Literally, "Spanish") Hebrew pronounciation is the norm.

Avot (H.) — Literally, "fathers," the sages who created the Talmud.

Baal Koreh (H.) — Literally, "Master of calling upon," the person who leads the prayers in a Jewish service. Not necessarily the Rabbi, especially in traditional Orthodox congregations.

Baal T'shuvah (H.) — Literally, "Master of return (repentance)." A Jew who has returned to strict halachic observance after having fallen away. The word t'shuvah, which means repentance, comes from the root meaning return; Judaism conceives of repentance as a return to a previous state of holiness which all persons are believed to possess.

Bat Mitzvah (H.) — Literally, "Daughter of the commandment," a ceremony for thirteen year old girls in which they attain the rights and responsibilities of Jewish adulthood. Parallel to the Bar Mitzvah for boys, and a more recent development. *Banot Mitzah* is the plural of Bat Mitzvah.

Bobe (Y.) — Grandmother.

B'reyshit (H.) — the first word of the Bible in Hebrew, "in the beginning." Also the Hebrew name of the book of Genesis.

Conservative Judaism — one of four streams of American Judaism. Less pure in its observance of the law, but less liberal and more rooted in Jewish norms than is Reform Judaism. Conservative Jews tend to follow some, but not all, of the laws and commandments, and may not do so consistently.

Daven (Y.) — To pray out loud.

Diaspora — any place outside of Israel to which Jews have been dispersed. In Hebrew, *Galut*, meaning exile.

Frummer (Y.) — from the Yiddish word "frum," strictly observant, a somewhat pejorative term used by Yiddish speakers to describe religious Jews.

Haftorah (H.) — Portions from the non-Torah parts of the Old Testament which teach parallel lessons to those found in Torah parshot. Haftorah reading was originally developed during periods of oppression in which Jews were forbidden to read the Torah out loud;

instead, Haftorah would be read in order to convey the same message. Haftorah portions are read by young girls being Bat Mitzvah in synagogue as the centerpiece of the Bat Mitzvah ritual. As with Torah parshot, each week has its own Haftorah parsha with special pieces for specific holidays.

Halacha (H.) — Literally, "The way of walking." A term which refers to the rules and norms of Jewish law. If something is "Halachically correct," it is precisely within the lines of Jewish law.

Haskalah (H.) — Literally, "Enlightenment," a period in the late 1700's and early 1800's in which a secular Judaism began to develop in Europe following Napoleon's emancipation of the Jews. Centered in Germany, the Austro-Hungarian Empire, and France.

Hassid (Y. and H.) — Literally, "righteous one," a follower of Hassidism, the mystical sect of Judaism founded by Israel Baal Shem Tov in the 1600's. One kind of ultraorthodox Jew.

Hillel (H.) — B'nai Brith Hillel is a campus Jewish student organization, and the main representative of mainstream Judaism on most college campuses. Provides social, recreational, and religious activities for Jewish students. Named for the great Jewish sage of the First Century, who was known for his compassion and concern for social justice.

Kadosh (H.) — Holy, or sanctified; the more literal Hebrew root refers to being set apart.

Kashrut (H.) — the dietary laws, observed by religious Jews. Basic precepts include never mixing meat with dairy, and not eating certain forbidden foods including pork, shellfish, and birds of prey. Also requires certain standards for slaughtering of animals and preparation of food so as to drain all blood from meat. These laws can be found in Parshat K'doshim.

Mikvah (H.) — the ritual bath in which women cleanse themselves after menstruation. Must contain "mayim chayim," living water, which is usually interpreted to mean rainwater.

Pale of Settlement — The part of Russia, consisting of territories belonging originally to Poland, Lithuania, the Ukraine, and Moldavia, in which Jews were required to live by Czarist edict; the place of origin of many Eastern European Jews who moved to North America. With few exceptions, Jewish subjects of the Czars were not permitted to live elsewhere in Russia, and Jews who had lived elsewhere were forcibly deported into this area.

Parshat K'doshim (H.) — In Jewish usage, the Torah is divided into sections called "Parsha." Each parsha is titled by its theme; one is read each week of the year on Sabbath during services, and there are special parshot for certain holy days. This portion, called "Holiness," contains the laws in which the Jews are commanded to be holy, or santified, by means of dietary, social, and sexual norms.

Pikuach nefesh (H.) — Literally, "The redemption of a soul," meaning the saving of a life. Halacha states that to save a life, almost any law may be broken, including the dietary laws and those governing the Sabbath.

Pilpul (H.) — The process of dialectical struggle and debate engaged in by Jewish scholars attempting to clarify points of the Law.

Pirke Avot (H.) — Literally, "Sayings of the Fathers." A collection of pithy sayings uttered by the sages who compiled the Talmud, the interpretation of Torah. These sayings tend to be exhortations to high standards of personal conduct and scholarship.

Rebbe (Y.) — Rabbi or teacher, the leader of a group of Hassidim.

Schul (Y.) — Literally "school," a place of learning; Synagogue.

Second Aliyah (H.) — Literally, the "going up," a term used to describe large-scale movements of immigration from Europe to Israel. A Jew always "goes up" to Israel, and "goes down" when leaving. The Second Aliyah refers to a specific historical period in the early 1900's in which idealistic young Jewish women and men moved to what was then Turkish Palestine to start Jewish settlements. These are the people who invented the Kibbutz.

Shabbat (H.) — The Sabbath. Observant Jews do not work on the Sabbath from sundown Friday night until sundown Saturday. Work has been defined in the interpretations of Jewish law as anything which changes the state or essence of a thing, and includes driving cars, using money, turning on the TV or electricity, and answering the phone.

Shoresh (H.) — The three-consonant root of a word in Hebrew. All Hebrew words contain such a root, which allows a scholar to trace its history entomologically and to determine its underlying meanings.

Talmud (H.) — The voluminous interpretations of the laws of the Torah. Originally oral traditions, the Talmud was codified over several centuries by collectives of sages who met and argued together about the correct meaning of Torah. Contains rules for daily application of the Law. The authoritative document of Jewish life.

Torah (H.) — First five books of the Old Testament. The Law. The most sacred scriptures of Judaism; Orthodox Jews believe they were given directly to the Jews by God. One common practice of anti-Semites over the ages has been to burn or desecrate Torah scrolls.

Trup (H.) — The special musical notation used in the chanting of Torah and Haftorah. Although the symbols look the same, different melodies are used for the chanting of each, and there are special melodies for the High Holy Days.

Vayikra (H.) — Literally, "And he called," the first word in the Book of Leviticus and the book's Hebrew name. Books of the Torah are referred to in Hebrew by their first word.

Workman's Circle — A socialist Jewish workers' organization which stressed the development of Yiddish culture and was not initially supportive of a Zionist and Hebrew-speaking perspective. Developed in Eastern Europe; in the U.S., supported fraternal organizations and Jewish cultural schools and events in which Yiddish was spoken.

Yiddishkeit (Y.) — Jewishness; refers to Eastern European Jewish cultural ways of being.

Zeyde (Y.) — Grandfather.

Reflections of a Jewish Lesbian-Feminist Activist-Therapist; Or, First of All I Am Jewish, the Rest Is Commentary

Adrienne J. Smith

> So it is better to speak
> remembering
> we were never meant to survive.
>
> Audre Lorde, 1978

This is a personal story of a life-long voyage toward lesbian and Jewish consciousness. My upbringing as a Jew was casual, to say the least. We did or did not go to a Reform Temple, depending on the weather, other commitments or sometimes just mood. We did or did not observe various holidays. In December we celebrated both Hanukkah and Christmas. I remember one year when there was a tree (an annual event) in the living room, a menorah in the dining room, and a ham being prepared in the kitchen. At 13 I was confirmed, not Bat Mitzvah.

But the Jewishness seeped through. Not in rituals and religion; to

Adrienne Smith, PhD, is a clinical psychologist in private practice. An early theorist in feminist therapy, she was a founding member of the Feminist Therapy Institute. Now middle-aged, she is the President of the American Psychological Association's Division 44, the Society for the Psychological Study of Lesbian and Gay Issues. She is pleased and grateful for her Jewish heritage.

this day I know almost no Hebrew and follow the prayers by mimicking others. It seeped through with German relatives who drifted through our house, refugees from Hitler (I realized later); with the unquestioned charity to those in need of a home, a meal or a job; with my father's hatred of Joe McCarthy combined with his pride that we lived in a country that allowed him to speak; with our support of the NAACP as well as the UJA.

The product of a German mother and a Russian father, both Jews, I also learned prejudice at home. My father, an uneducated immigrant, was never seen by my mother and her family as the equal of my American-born and college-educated mother. In attempting to identify with both I learned how to be both oppressed and oppressor. Later that expanded to an awareness of myself as a member of a persecuted minority — Jewish — with a pride in special ability and sensitivity, also Jewish. The messages about my safety as a Jew were also mixed. I grew up in a Jewish family in a Jewish neighborhood and so was protected. At the same time Hitler was rampaging through Europe, and Israel did not yet exist. Thus, while I was comfortable and accepted locally, in the wider world we were everywhere in danger. I learned about the "we" as a Jew, not only internationally but historically. We were persecuted everywhere and had been for all time.

I learned early about being an invisible member of a minority. My name, together with my blonde hair and blue eyes, led to frequent assumptions that I was not Jewish. As an undergraduate in downstate Illinois I was challenged to prove I was Jewish by a farm girl who had never seen a Jew before. Even when I worked for a rabbi, a surprised temple member who met me exclaimed, "I didn't know the temple hired non-Jewish workers." Despite the Mogen David I now wear, this assumption is still made.

As I reached 40 and beyond I sought out more understanding of my roots and greater identification as a Jew. I visited Israel, read books such as "World of our Fathers" (sic!) (Howe, 1976) and "Life is with People" (Zborowski, 1962) and talked incessantly about being Jewish. As a middle-aged woman, my life-focus has increasingly turned from career development to a desire to be part of a community and a tradition. Feminism, lesbianism and Jewishness, each in its own way, provides such community.

Not until I came out publicly as a lesbian and, despite my traditional training, began to identify myself as a feminist therapist, however, did I become aware of just how much my Jewishness meant to me and for me. By acknowledging membership in a persecuted minority and by publicly espousing radical ideas within my profession of psychology the unspoken values and the world view I had absorbed as a Jew became increasingly salient.

For me, being a feminist therapist reflects many Jewish values. One of the central concepts of feminist therapy is empowerment (Smith & Douglas, 1990). While Judaism is not necessarily anti-authoritarian, the central belief is that each man (sic!) can speak directly to God without a priestly intermediary. In fact, it is imperative — for males — that literacy in the Torah, the ability both to read and to discuss various meanings and interpretations, be demonstrated (through the Bar Mitzvah) before a boy is granted full adult status in the Jewish community. Ten of these literate adult males can then gather and have a prayer service without a leader or rabbi. Rabbis serve as community leaders and teachers but they are not the route to God. (See end note.)

This basic tenet of Judaism, then, that each person is responsible for his (sic) own relationship with God, when expanded to include women and all people, means each of us has the same potential power and we can each, on our own, reach the goals we set without depending on someone else who is more learned or more blessed. Empowerment, then, is simply the job I do as a therapist to help my clients remove whatever obstacles prevent them from knowing and using their own power. And, not surprisingly, I often use books, fiction, non-fiction and poetry, as therapeutic tools. As in Jewish tradition where children are expected to acquire the skills and learning to become adult members of the community, feminist therapy expects clients to be capable of running their own lives without dependence on outside authority.

From the same root comes the well known Jewish maxim, "Three Jews, four opinions." As individual thinkers who delight in philosophical argument (pilpul) we are keenly aware that there are many ways to see each issue, many truths, many ways to live a life. This allows me, as a therapist, to counter the rigidly held beliefs in absolute right and wrong with which my clients often torture themselves. Frequently clients take the first step in recognizing buried anger or ambivalent feelings toward a parent in response to my suggesting that there are other ways to interpret an event.

"If I am not for myself, who will be for me?"

This, the first line of the famous saying by Rabbi Hillel, encapsulates a great deal of the work I do with women who have been taught that they must sacrifice themselves for others' needs. I interpret Hillel in two ways, both of which, in my view, are major components of therapy. First, we must take care of our own needs since no one else will. This, of course, includes learning to be aware of our needs, to honor them and to articulate them clearly, and to learn to recognize when they are not being met. Second, I add the word "responsible" to the saying, thus: "If I am not responsible for myself, who will be responsible for me?" Once we as women have learned to ask for our needs we must deal with acting responsibly. Actually, I focus on taking authorship and therefore responsibility for our own actions throughout therapy but this becomes increasingly important as women become more direct in their communications. The message I get from Hillel and that I try to transmit is that taking care of ourselves and our needs is not an act of selfishness but of responsibility. Only to the extent that we are willing to take responsibility for our own lives, can we then act responsibly towards others.

"If I am only for myself, what am I?"

The second line of Hillel's saying is a direct call to social action. While most forms of therapy concentrate on the individual, feminist therapy is constantly aware of the embeddedness of each person's life within a social context and of the responsibility of each individual to act for the good of the community. Feminist therapists themselves are frequently social activists. Indeed, the Feminist Therapy Ethical Code (1987) demands a proactive stance toward the solution of social injustices. Although my clients are under no obligation to follow my example as an activist, they are aware of my values and of my strongly held belief that we must join with like-minded others to "change the world."

"If not now, when?"

This last line of Hillel's saying sums up the Jewish view of the afterlife in four words. And by implication Hillel also is telling us to live life to its fullest now and not to put off helping ourselves and others to achieve as much joy as possible. In my therapeutic work clients are encouraged to try new ways of approaching problems throughout therapy rather than waiting until they are finished or until they feel less frightened or more skilled. They are not pressured to do something until they feel ready but, conversely, they are not urged to put off experimenting until some future perfection is reached. Life is short and precious; we do not have all eternity in which either to reap the rewards for a life of self-sacrifice or to pay with regrets for a life of self-indulgence. Rewards, punishments, regrets and celebrations are all part of the now, to be experienced directly in the present.

It is not only my identity and functioning as a therapist that is rooted in my Jewishness; my lesbian activism is as well. While the influences on my therapeutic theory and practice are based primarily in the teachings of Judaism, the Jewish foundation of my activism comes from my sense of identity as a Jew and the emotional understandings and responses I have acquired as part of a cultural and ethnic group. The consciousness I developed as a member of one minority group translates almost directly as I have recognized my membership in other minority groups.

One of my most basic identities as a Jew is a sense of sharing with an entire people, of being part of a community made up of millions of others no matter how scattered geographically, and of a tradition which includes all my ancestors and descendants. For Jews this sense of connection is reinforced continually, perhaps most dramatically in the yearly Passover story which states "WE were slaves in Egypt" (not "they," as part of the story explains). In less formal but no less pervasive a fashion, many Jews, in one way or another, respond to major news items with the fearful thought, "is this good or bad for the Jews?"

While as a Jew I always felt myself to be part of a community, my first consciousness of being a lesbian was of being different in a very negative and a very isolated manner. Since I became aware of my lesbianism quite a few years before the Stonewall "riot"—the event which sparked the current gay rights movement—the search for others like myself was furtive and frustrating. Where were my contemporaries? Who in history had been lesbian or homosexual? I read medical texts, sleazy novels, and homophobic biographies. Aside from my lover, I knew only a handful of other lesbians and gay men. All of us lived in fear that the "wrong" people would find out. It was not until the birth of the gay rights movement that the "we" took shape and I had others with whom to interact openly.

Almost immediately I began to assess the costs and privileges of being visible. For me, the cost of continuing to hide my lesbianism after many years in the closet had simply become more than I could bear. The need to pass, to use cover stories or twist pronouns, to pretend to a life I did not live and to not acknowledge the life I lived had begun to subvert my sense of identity as a human being and to undermine my worth as a person. I left my establishment job, came out publicly and almost instantly became involved in activist organizations.

After years of feeling isolated, the joy of again being part of a community propelled me into activism. As a Jew, the certain knowledge that I am part of a larger whole, that I am not alone even at my most lonely, that I can travel anywhere in the world and establish connection with other Jews has come to parallel the identical sense I now have that I am part of the larger lesbian and gay community.

During the past several years my activism has been focussed almost entirely within my profession of psychology, specifically in the lesbian/gay movement within the American Psychological Association. It is through my work with this group that I have become aware of the similarities between the lesbian/gay activist community and the Jewish community. There are three elements that are part of what I call "the Jewish character" that are for me the same as elements of the "lesbian/gay activist character." The first of these is the one I have been emphasizing and which I see as basic to activism, that is, a deep sense of community, even of family, which enables members of a group to see themselves as part of a larger whole with the continuity of tradition and history. One of the first results of Stonewall in 1969 and of the creation of the Association of [Lesbian and] Gay Psychologists in 1973 was an end to isolation and an identification with a community larger than oneself. My Jewish sense that we are all responsible for each other and for the survival of our culture is reflected in the activist's awareness that we are working for each other and for the young people who will follow us. As activists, we are very conscious that we must build our own "family" since frequently our families of origin have shut us out. This is much the same as the Jewish response of building our own communities after various nations denied us participation in their communal life.

The second similar element is a knowledge that we are working/ fighting for our lives. To be a Jew or a lesbian/gay activist is to be aware that our freedom, our rights, our very existence is threatened constantly by enemies who see us as less than human. For any reason or for no reason whatever we can be deprived of our homes or our jobs. Our reputations can be attacked; indeed our very bodies can be subject to violent physical attack. Since our survival depends on the success of our work as activists, we work with incredible intensity and dedication. And, again like Jews, we monitor our world continually for indications of homophobia and respond immediately with as much strength as we can muster.

The third element, and the one without which none of us could continue to function, is the sheer joy, exuberance and sensuality of working within the lesbian/gay activist community in psychology. Eastern European Jews, with whose cultural tradition I identify, are frequently depicted as celebrating life and their ability to survive, as taking pleasure in whatever life offers and in finding the absurd even in difficult circumstances. Perhaps the most easily available expression of this approach to life is "Fiddler on the Roof" but any of Sholem Alecheim's stories or Marc Chagall's paintings also demonstrates it. In my experience of lesbian/gay activism there has been, from the beginning, marvelous combinations of seriousness and humor. The underlying structure of gay/lesbian life styles and therefore activism is the same as that of feminism, that is, the questioning of "standard" gender roles. In activism this translates into an ability to act playfully, to deal with sex, gender and social norms humorously. No one is expected to "act like a lady" or to be "a real man." Much of this humor is of the type known as "gender-bending": some of it is designed to unsettle the assumptions of masculine and feminine behavior of our more "establishment" colleagues.

Within our lesbian/gay activist group, both women and men are free to hug, to share feelings, to cry together and laugh together, to act assertively or emphatically, and, not least, (with thanks to Emma Goldman) to dance together.

As I look back on this journey of self-discovery, I realize that coming out as a lesbian was, in large part, the stimulus to coming out as a Jew. Gay pride, the result of reclaiming a stigmatized identity and redefining oneself, has led to Jewish pride so that over time I have embraced all my identities. The joyous release of energy when no part of oneself needs to be hidden is beautifully documented in two recent books, *Nice Jewish Girls* (Beck, 1982) and *Twice Blessed* (Balka & Rose, 1989) which celebrate combining our Jewish and lesbian/gay selves.

As I became aware of the almost universal heterosexual assumptions of our society I also became aware of its equally pervasive "Christian" assumptions. This assumption of commonality with the dominant culture not only denies identity to the individual but denies uniqueness to the group and culture as well. Redefining this uniqueness as an enriching heritage rather than a despised difference, celebrating my identity as a member of an outsider culture, means celebrating the survival of a group that was, as Audre Lorde said, "never meant to survive."

NOTE

It is important to make note of the many Jewish feminists who are working to change the liturgy and to include rather than exclude women in all aspects of Jewish religious and scholarly life.

REFERENCES

Balka, C. & Rose, A. (Eds.) (1989). *Twice blessed: On being lesbian, gay and Jewish*. Boston: Beacon Press.

Beck, E.T. (Ed.) (1982). *Nice Jewish girls: A lesbian anthology*. Watertown, MA: Persephone Press.

Feminist Therapy Institute (1987). *Feminist therapy ethical code*. Pasadena, CA. (Available from FTI Administrative Office, 904 Irving St., #258, San Francisco, CA 94122).

Howe, I. (1976). *World of our fathers*. New York: Harcourt Brace Jovanovitch.

Lorde, A. (1978). A litany for survival. In A. Lorde, *The black unicorn*. New York: W. W. Norton.

Smith, A.J. & Douglas, M.A. (1990). Empowerment as the central ethical imperative in feminist therapy. In H. Lerman, & N. Porter, (Eds.), *Ethics in feminist therapy*. New York: Springer.

Zborowski, M. (1962). *Life is with people: The culture of the shtetl*. New York: Schocken Books.

The Missing

They lie legs entwined in the dawn's early light
    and tears are permitted.
This is the century where we do not weep for loss
    but cry at the return.

They will, at 5 A.M., descend
to a cold dawn airport & champagne
in an overheated waiting room.
At 11 A.M. they will walk down the avenue:
balloons, streamers, keys to the city!

I want to see headlines that say:
all the Jews came home —
the Film reversed, smoke curled back,
yellow vacuumed into grey stone chimneys,
gold returned to teeth —
flesh & clothes back on the bodies.

Erased from ordinary days:
among neighbors with shared weather,
sewer & traffic problems, a loose fence,
a lost barking dog, shared sleep-over
children — They were torn
into a time-hole.
Some awoke, dressed for work & after coffee
take a tree-lined walk into sudden cold,
damp stone floors . . . the hatred of strangers.

From that place without clocks the trip is booked
through Russian-Polish camps, Haitian suburbs,
embassies in Beirut, ditches in El Salvador.
The "missing" are found in the trunk of a car
on a Roman street or shackled in an American
mall-town cellar. In Germany
they packed them in cattle cars.

But sometimes they return on the Greyhound bus:
To Central Avenue, the 3rd house on the left
(with the basket-ball hoop in the driveway).
The neighbors have brought baked ham,
macaroni salad, carrot-spice cake —
there is champagne won and saved
for all the sea of talk.
And when they stop and leave at 1:30 A.M.,
when the dog's been out, the cat is in
and the kids have been carried to sleep,
then the miracle will occur.

Bodies will be reunited —
In the now warm bed with the wedding quilt
it will be as if it had never happened.
As if it could not happen.

— Mira J. Spektor

Mira J. Spektor is a poet, composer and music director of the Aviva Players, a group that has specialized, since 1975, in the works of Women Composers. Her poems have appeared in *Seems* and *Rhino*, as well as Haworth Press, Inc. publications. As a composer, her work includes two chamber operas, a feminist musical (*The Housewives' Cantata*), and music for film and television. Born in Europe, she graduated from Sarah Lawrence College, lives in New York City, and has two grandchildren.

Clearance Sale

To Max Hamburger*

Thousands of suitcases,
shoes, eyeglasses,
wigs, hair
heaped in piles
Life in Auschwitz
was like a clearance sale

—Miriam L. Vogel

Miriam Lea Vogel, MSW, is a feminist therapist in private practice in Seattle. Born in Amsterdam, the Netherlands, in 1944, her poetry has been an important way to address the meaning of the Holocaust in her life and the lives of her family and friends. She sees poetry as a part of the therapy and healing process.

---

*Max Hamburger survived Auschwitz against all odds. After the war he became a psychiatrist who worked with survivors and the children of survivors. Now in his seventies he teaches Jews and non-Jews about discrimination and its consequences in a reconstructed synagogue in the south of Holland.

But You Don't Look Jewish!

Rita Arditti

As an Argentinean Sephardic Jew* who has lived most of her life
in non-Sephardic communities, I have come to recognize that my
identity and personality have been, to a significant degree, shaped
by my ethnic/cultural background. My experience as a psychotherapy client has led me to believe that one's cultural and ethnic background is an essential part of the context of therapy and need always
to be taken into account.

When I mention that I am a Jew, people often look at me with
surprise and emphatically exclaim, "But you don't look Jewish!" I
then explain that I am a Sephardic Jew, born in Argentina of Turkish immigrant parents whose ancestors were expelled from Spain in
1492, when Spain became a Catholic country again after several
centuries of Moslem rule. My being very specific about my family
origins helps people understand who I am, and enables me to maintain a stronger sense of self when communicating with others.

Recently I had a conversation with an Ashkenazi** Jewish couple about the Palestinian uprising and the Israeli government's re-

Rita Arditti was born in Argentina to a Jewish Sephardic family. She has a
doctorate in Biology, and has co-edited two books, *Science and Liberation* (South
End Press, 1980) and *Test-Tube Women — What Future for Motherhood*? (Pandora
Press, 1984, 1989). She is one of the founders of *New Words*, a women's book-
store in Cambridge, MA, and is on the faculty of the Graduate Program of the
Union Institute.

*Sephardic Jews are Jews of Spanish and Portugese descent. The term comes
from *Sepharad* — the Hebrew name for Spain. However, the term is sometimes
also used to include Jews from the Middle East, Asia and Africa. In this article, I
use the term in its most literal sense.

**Ashkenazi Jews are Jews from Germany and Eastern Europe. Yiddish is the
language of the Ashkenazim.

sponse to it. I could feel that some of my critical comments about Israel were not being well received. One of my interlocutors looked me straight in the eye and stated forcefully that whenever wrong things happen, Jews are blamed for them. Not wanting to escalate the discussion into an argument, I retreated into silence for a moment. Then, almost casually, I mentioned that I was a Sephardic Jew and that my family also had relatives living in Israel. Immediately, the mood of the conversation changed. They now, in a friendly manner, asked questions regarding my cultural background and personal history. My previous comments were no longer seen as antiSemitic.

I left that conversation with mixed feelings. While glad that we had reached a more meaningful level of communication, I was also once again reminded that most people, Jews and non-Jews, are often totally oblivious to the existence of the Sephardim.

I started to explore my own origins about twelve years ago. I was motivated by the gnawing sense of "differentness" I felt when in the company of Ashkenazi Jews, both in Argentina and in the United States. I could not understand why I felt so different from other middle class Jews and in the beginning I attributed this feeling to personal idiosyncrasies. When my attempts to sort out what I thought were just individual differences didn't provide an adequate explanation, I started reading and reflecting about the different historical and cultural circumstances that had shaped my experience growing up in a large, tight-knit Sephardic community in Argentina.

As I started to put the pieces together, I began to realize that part of my sense of self derives from Sephardic Jewish history; that history shapes how I feel and how I interpret the world. Not everything can be explained by idiosyncrasies! The anger and pain that I had felt about my marginality started to go away. By delving into the incredibly rich and exciting history of the Sephardim, I developed a keen sense of wonder about my heritage.*

---

*For more information about Sephardic history, see the list "Resources on the Sephardim" in my article, "To be a Hanu" (pp. 16-26) in *The Tribe of Dina—A Jewish Women's Anthology*, edited by Melanie Kaye/Kantrowitz and Irena Klepfisz, Beacon Press, 1989.

Generally, accounts of Jewish history present the Sephardim as playing a minor and secondary role. Media presentations about the Holocaust make no mention of the Sephardic communities that were destroyed, such as Salonika in Greece or Bitola in Yugoslavia, or of Sephardim survivors of the Holocaust. I was very moved when I learned recently that in Bitola there is a bust of a Jewish partisan heroine who perished fighting near the Yugoslav-Greek border. Her name was Estreya Ovadia (*The Sephardic Home News,* 1983). The image of a Sephardic woman being a freedom fighter during World War II was totally new to me.

In the United States, Ashkenazi Jews have made their mark in the arts, in the professions, and in the sciences. Yiddish expressions have become part of American culture (at least in places with large Ashkenazi populations) and Broadway musicals and Hollywood movies have immortalized Eastern European Jews (*Fiddler on the Roof, Yentl,* etc.). The Israeli government is overwhelmingly composed of Ashkenazi Jews in spite of the fact that the majority of the population is not Ashkenazim. This situation reinforces the sense that the Ashkenazim are the most important Jews.

The invisibility of Sephardim in American history is ironic, as there are many intimate connections between Sephardic and early American history. The same day that the Spanish Jews were forced to leave Spain (the first day of August, 1492), Christopher Columbus was also scheduled to leave Spain. He had to use the port of Palos because "the more convenient port of Cadiz was too crowded with hapless Jews praying that the expulsion order would be rescinded" (Feingold, 1982, p. 3). Historians have long debated whether Columbus had Jewish ancestry. However that question is resolved, it is a fact that Columbus's voyage would not have taken place without the influence and money of his *Converso** backers. Furthermore, his second trip was "financed from confiscated Jewish property, including the sale of precious religious objects" (Feingold, 1982, p. 5). Jews also contributed to the nautical technology that made his voyages possible. Spanish Jews often acted as

---

Conversos were Jews who became Christians outwardly but continued practicing Judaism in secret. They were under constant scrutiny from the Inquisition.

intellectual bridges, bringing technology and ideas from the Greeks and the Arabs into the Christian world.

The history of the Jewish community in the United States began with the arrival, by a fluke of history, of twenty-three Sephardic Jews in September, 1654. These Jews came from Recife, Brazil, trying to escape the Inquisition, after the Dutch administration was defeated by the Portuguese. They were expelled from Brazil and set out for Holland in a convoy of sixteen ships. Fifteen of these ships arrived at their destination but one was blown off course and captured by Spanish pirates. These Sephardim, held to be sold as slaves, were eventually rescued and taken to New Amsterdam. How they managed to stay and survive in spite of the hostility of Peter Stuyvesant, the governor of New Amsterdam, who asked them to leave, is a fascinating chapter of American and Jewish history (Dimont, 1978).

It is not surprising, then, given the history of the Sephardim, that the theme of "expulsion" is a central one in our culture. When, as a child, I asked where our family came from, why my relatives spoke Ladino* and why so few people knew about this language, the first explanation my parents offered was always the banishment from Spain. This episode, dating 500 years earlier, was supposed to answer my questions and explain our situation. It was an ever-present theme and the emotions connected with it were complex. Certainly part of the message was that since exile was a common occurrence in Sephardic history, it could happen again. But also there was a sense of pride associated with that event: our ancestors had been expelled because they refused to renounce their faith. They had been true to their origins and loyal to their culture. They were, above all, Jews who would go to any extremes to maintain their Jewishness. I learned that we, their descendants, were expected to do the same, even if sometimes we could not articulate or agree on what that meant.

Personally, I know that one of the reasons I decided to become a U.S. citizen instead of remaining a permanent resident alien

---

*Ladino is the language of the Sephardim, which is fifteenth-century Spanish with local words of the places where the Sephardim went into exile and some Hebrew. It is also known as *Judezmo*, or Judeo-Spanish.

was that a little voice inside me would sometimes whisper "expulsion . . ." While I did not consciously think that I ever would be deported for being a Sephardic Jew, I have always been keenly aware of the possibility of deportation for political activities, more so than many of my friends who were also foreigners and who shared similar political perspectives.

In addition to commitment and pride, hope and endurance were emotional qualities instilled in the Sephardim over the course of our history. The Jews left Spain hoping that one day they would be allowed back. The story goes that they took with them the keys to their houses, and passed these from parents to children, through generations, waiting for the day when the keys would be used to return to their homes. It is claimed that, indeed, when some Jews went back after centuries, their keys still fit the doors of their houses.

Endurance has been an ever present theme through Sephardic history. The Sephardim always stress that Sephardic culture did not disappear, that though our ancestors integrated themselves very successfully in the countries that received them, they kept their language, their music, and their traditions. This ability to persist and the refusal to blur differences has always been considered a strength, and proof of resilience and integrity. Many times I have heard approving comments regarding the "stubbornness" and uniqueness of the Sephardim.

These qualities—commitment, pride, endurance and hope—that stem from our history have influenced me, and I recognize them as part of my emotional make-up. Particularly, the abilities to persist in difficult circumstances and to derive strength from a long-range perspective seem to be characteristics I have "inherited" from my background.

These qualities played a crucial role in helping me carve a life for myself that was very different from what was expected from me as a Sephardic woman. In my family, all the women were housewives and mothers. Only one of my mother's sisters, who was considered "peculiar," worked outside of the home. We, the daughters, were supposed to get married soon after high school, have children and live our lives in the context of the Sephardic community. I still remember the puzzled look on my father's face when I announced that I planned to go to the university. The belief that "home and family" ought to be the primary focus of Sephardic women's lives is deeply embedded in the culture. When it became clear to me that I wanted a different life, I felt quite isolated from other Sephardim and fantasized that Ashkenazi women had an easier time in moving into the wider world. This, undoubtedly, contributed to my sense of "differentness" from them.

As a feminist, I particularly relate to the Kabbala, the mystical body of Jewish thought and learning that flourished in Spain and was later developed by Sephardic Rabbis in Palestine, since it is one of the few sources of Judaism that acknowledges the power of the female. According to the Kabbala, one of the causes of human suffering is the alienation of the masculine from the feminine in God, the alienation of God and the Shekinah (the feminine aspect of God); the world will not be whole until this split is healed. I resonate with this view. I also feel a special connection to the Kabbala because one of the leading Kabbalists in the sixteenth century was Moshe ben Yaakov Cordovero, most likely an ancestor on my mother's side of the family. My mother's name was Rosa Cordovero and her family came from Cordoba.

One observation that I have made about the Sephardim that I have not been able to explain satisfactorily and that still amazes me is the following: the Sephardim have an uncanny, almost eerie, ability to recognize each other. Because, after the expulsion, the Sephardim dispersed widely in many different countries (Holland, England, Turkey, Italy, Greece, etc.), they have been exposed to many and varied cultural influences. However, Sephardim from different countries can easily recognize each other with almost total certainty. I first thought that this was my own unique ability, the result of an inquisitive mind, but then I discovered that this is a common occurrence among the Sephardim. The explanation for this phenomenon is not clear to me. I like to think that, because as a group we have been so marginalized and fragmented, we have developed special skills to recognize each other, to help us survive, to find others like us and to reconnect.

Our collective memory has also played a central role in keeping us alive. Historical memory is the antidote to invisibility. We have had to look back in time to get images that reinforce and help us understand our social identity. As an individual, in looking for ways to connect with my background, especially while in therapy, I explored the memories of my childhood. There are close to half a million Jews in Argentina; it is the fifth largest Jewish community in the world. Of these, between 70,000 and 90,000 are Sephardim. Growing up in a Jewish household, playing with my numerous cousins and sisters, I did not meet non-Jewish and Ashkenazi children until I went to school, so my early memories were completely embedded in Sephardic culture. When I first met an Ashkenazi Jewish girl, at school, I did not believe she could be a Jew; and I know she felt the same about me. Religious holidays with a large family, Sephardic foods and Ladino sayings framed my childhood.

Ladino is a very expressive and genteel language whose real flavor, unfortunately, is lost in translation. The power of language became clear to me when I realized that whole categories of experience and early recollections could be suddenly awakened by hearing Ladino. Just a few words of Ladino could bring back scenes and moods which I had completely forgotten. Ladino proverbs and sayings (which are countless), short and to the point, were specially effective in provoking a groundswell of memories.

My personal identity, then, is rooted in my early history and in the identity of the group into which I was born. Only when I was able to make these connections could I understand some of the forces that shaped my life and influenced my choices. For me, my Sephardic identity is not different from my Jewish identity; they are one and the same.

When I identify myself as a Sephardic Jew, I want people to know my background and to appreciate the particular characteristics that have been essential to the survival of the Sephardim. One of these is the ability to move between cultures and to have practical strategies for living within different communities. It is common, for instance, for Sephardic Jews to know many languages. I think of my father who, as a young man with very little formal education, went to Argentina and used his knowledge of Spanish, Ladino, Turkish, French, Hebrew and some Greek to carve a position for himself in the import-export textile business. This ability to travel and to learn languages requires an attitude of acceptance and awareness of the wider world that was essential to our survival. I consider myself fortunate to be part of that heritage. It helps me explain how I came alone to the United States when I was eighteen years old, went to Italy when I was twenty and lived there for ten years, and returned to the United States when I was thirty-two. In the process I learned Italian, French, and English.

But while I was able to adapt easily to any language or country, over time I became less connected to my roots and began to feel a sense of loss. In therapy, I was fortunate to have an intelligent and sensitive therapist who asked probing questions about my background and helped me reconnect and recognize long buried parts of myself. Lacking an Argentinean Sephardic environment in my current situation, I turned to Ladino songs and proverbs, and to traditional foods, for catalysts to remembering.

If I were to give some suggestions for therapists, I would recommend that clients be asked about their cultural and religious backgrounds. They should be asked about the attitudes toward women in their cultures of origin and about the impact they think those attitudes have had on their lives. If they are Jews, it should not be assumed that they are Ashkenazim; if they are Sephardim, it is important to find out about their language of origin and their particular history (of course this applies also to Jews from the Middle East, Asia and Africa). If they are Hispanic Catholic, the therapist should be aware that there might be some Converso experience in their backgrounds.*

To deny our history is to obliterate an incredibly important part of the Jewish experience in the world and to collude with the stereotyped assumptions that are made about Jews. The lack of images of Sephardic Jews in mainstream and in Jewish culture in the United States contributes to our invisibility. The Sephardim in the United States constitute a tiny minority of about 150,000, living primarily in New York, Los Angeles, Seattle and Atlanta. As a result, it is fairly easy for people to forget about our existence. Not being rec-

---

*The *cheutas*, Catholic descendants of converted families who live on the island Palma de Majorca, still suffer discrimination and are reluctant to discuss their background. The same is true of the descendants of Spanish Jews in New Mexico and southern Colorado. See "The Crypto Jews," National Public Radio "All Things Considered" program # 880331, 1988, prepared by Benjamin Shapiro.

ognized as a Jew means I have often witnessed antiSemitic statements "from inside." When I protest and identify myself as a Jew, I am often told that I am "different" from those "penny-pinching Jews" with Russian-sounding names who are the real Jews.

And indeed, when I married an Ashkenazi Jew, I did feel that I was becoming more "legitimate" as a Jew and that I had gone a step up in the ladder of Jewishness. I could well understand the experience of the Sephardic woman I met on a trip to Israel, who told me that her family had been in Israel for centuries and spoke both Ladino and Hebrew, but she felt she needed to learn Yiddish in order to feel like a real Jew!

The Iberian Jews peacefully coexisted for 500 years with Christians and Muslims in a brilliant civilization that blended cultures, bloodlines and religions. I like to think that the worldliness which the history of the Sephardim exemplifies could help break barriers between Jews and non-Jews. Maintaining one's history and traditions while allowing for enrichment from other cultures can help to create a world where sectarianism could not thrive. This seems, in our times, an absolutely essential quality to ensure that humankind will have a future. I want more people to be aware of the existence of the Sephardim. It helps me as a person, in order to be seen and understood more clearly, but I also feel it is important for all Jews, as a group, to be aware of the cultural richness of the Sephardim. The Sephardic heritage belongs to all the Jewish people. We need to acknowledge it and preserve it for our own mental health and for the sake of the Jewish community at large.

REFERENCES

Dimont, M.I. (1978). *The Jews in America: The roots, history and destiny of American Jews*. NY: Simon and Schuster.

Feingold, H.L. (1982). *A Midrash on American Jewish history*. Albany: State University of New York Press.

The Sephardic Home News (1983, March). "Jews of Bitola remembered," pp. 1, 7 (article unsigned).

A Feminist Perspective on Intermarriage

Amy Sheldon

"If I am not for myself who is for me? And when I am for myself what am I? And if not now, when?" These well-known calls to consciousness and conscience are from the Jewish sage, Hillel (cited in Herford, 1962). They capture something important as I reflect on what it has been like to be a Jewish woman who is married to a nonJewish man. Hillel's words are familiar to every child who has a Jewish education. They are meaningful words that remain with me from mine. They are meant to stir the listener to action, to good deeds. I am stirred to write.

These words frame my intermarriage experience. They capture my sense of isolation and apprehension as a Jew who has done something that is taboo—marrying outside of my tribe. I was not ready for the messages that I got from my own people, that they were writing me off as a Jew, that they were not expecting me to continue to be a Jew, that they would even have trouble seeing my children as Jews. It is hard to live with the idea that a whole community is capable of automatically turning against me and my family. I had never before experienced ostracism from sister/fellow Jews. So Hillel's words captured for me the reality that I experienced early on, of a terrible struggle that I embarked on when I got married, and consequently, of powerful antagonistic feelings and apprehensions that I became aware of in myself and in the Jewish

Amy Sheldon is on the faculties of the Center for Advanced Feminist Studies and the Department of Linguistics, at the University of Minnesota, Minneapolis. Her research is concerned with ways in which children's conversations are gendered.

This paper is dedicated to Rene Schwartz. Thanks are due to Ellen Cole, Loraine Obler, and Rachel Josefowitz Siegel for their helpful comments on an earlier version.

79

community. Out of this cauldron of feelings and thoughts, I and my husband make decisions that have shaped our family and our reality.

My husband-to-be was a man who I felt connected to spiritually. In addition, he really wanted to be a father (not just to father) and he valued family. I also was intrigued by what seemed to be a simpler connection that he had to his religion, Catholicism, than I felt toward mine. He could pray. He enjoyed the liturgy. He sang it with feeling. I was moved by hymns he would play for me, at first on the piano, and then on the organ of an ornate church.

While I was drawn to his spirituality, I also deeply wanted to pray Jewishly, to find a Jewish spiritual expression. But I couldn't. I felt that I didn't know how. For one thing, I didn't know a lot of the Hebrew words, and I didn't understand much of the service when I heard it. I began to make some progress in prayer, when I courageously asked a local rabbi, "How does a person pray?" He said, "You just start." I understood his answer, and slowly I started, without worrying about form. It was working, and I felt drawn into my Judaism as a way to express my spirituality. But I also continued to feel blocked. At the time I attributed it to my ignorance and lack of practice. However, I have come to see that my block is not due to my own inadequacies. I just can't relate to the male-centered content and practice of traditional Judaism. I can't find myself in it. And I can't put myself in it. It has taken me a long time to realize the magnitude of this problem.

So for a long time the emerging religious expression I was giving to my spiritual longing has felt very fragile. Even so, my spirituality is strongly identified with being Jewish and being part of the Jewish community, even if I do not always express it in a synagogue.

My Jewish spirituality contributes to my struggle as an intermarried woman. As a Jew, I have experienced antiSemitism. I also know about attempts to destroy the Jews throughout history. But I always thought the destructiveness came from outside the Jewish community, from nonJews. I wasn't prepared, and didn't expect, to be hurt by other Jews. Although my family and friends have always been, and continue to be, extremely supportive of the person I was to marry, some other Jewish acquaintances have not been. The rabbi that I had dared to talk to about prayer would not marry us. "I can't," he said regretfully, "it is not allowed in Orthodox Judaism." A legalism. It hurt very much.

My grandfather, who died when I was a teenager, was Orthodox. Some of my clearest and most powerful feelings about being Jewish come from memories of seders and sabbath dinners in my grandparents' home. My grandfather used to cover my head with his hands and murmur a blessing whose words I did not understand, words which were never explained to me, but which told me he cared about me in a particular and mysterious way.

Many other of my childhood experiences intimately connected me with Jewish culture. I lived in a Jewish neighborhood in the Bronx, New York, a city which I experienced as being dominated by Jewish culture. On the Jewish High Holy days, the whole neighborhood was transformed. The elementary school that my friends and I attended was closed. Stores were closed. People dressed up. Activity was focused on the many shuls (synagogues) we could walk to. People congregated at the shuls, in the nearby parks, on the streets, spending the day in and out of shul, chatting and visiting with each other. There was a warmth and solidarity that as a child I didn't even call by name. It just enveloped me and sustained me and I flourished in it. It was like the communal smell of chicken soup and shabbos (sabbath) cooking that met me when I entered the cool marble lobby of my apartment building on a Friday afternoon.

The search for words and activities that can reweave the fabric of a Jewish childhood and consciously name and recreate that world comes as an adult. And it comes with a different kind of urgency and poignancy when one has a family of one's own, and sees how fragile life is. The world of our childhood no longer exists for us as adults. Many buildings in my old neighborhood have been boarded up or torn down. The neighborhood has been transformed by people who have another language and culture. My grandfather's tiny shul is now a church.

What does this have to do with intermarriage? Everything. What, after all, is marriage and having a family? It is a stage of personal evolution. One evolves from somewhere. That somewhere is one's childhood and subsequent life experiences. I see my search for self-expression in Judaism as a way to preserve the continuity of the fabric of my childhood in a world that keeps drastically changing.

One of those changes is the physical appearance of what I knew as "my neighborhood." Another is that many of my relatives are gone. The tradition of Judaism remains. But I can't embrace it fully unless it is transformed by Jewish women who speak to us too.

My search for a connection to Judaism that is right for me, my desire to protect my nourishing marital relationship, my personal sense of the injustice of the Orthodox Jewish legal system, my desire not to assimilate, my worry over the vulnerability of my young children to the Jewish community's insensitivity to or intolerance of intermarriage — all of these pressures left me feeling extremely vulnerable. For a long time I felt that there were no resources that I could turn to for support and guidance. I was repeatedly exposed to misunderstandings and put-downs because of the marriage choice that I had made.

Rejection and insensitivity from other Jews came early in my marriage. At lunch one day, I was having a conversation with a local feminist Jewish scholar who was a member of the women's minyan (feminist prayer group). I greatly admired her. I was in the early stages of pregnancy. I was conscious of creating new life. It was an especially joyful time for my husband and me, and also one filled with uncertainties and changes. Discussing Jewish intermarriage and families, she stated with an air of authority that most children of intermarriages were lost to the Jewish community and were not raised to be Jews. I thought to myself, "But that's not my case." She seemed to think that every such child in any family or community had the same probability of not being raised Jewishly. Again, as with the rabbi's refusal to marry us, I felt written off by one of my own people. I was astonished and unprepared. I felt totally adrift and very uncertain about what resources, both within and outside of myself, there might be to support me at my present stage of awareness and commitment to Judaism and to my future child's Jewishness. I felt unequipped to do the job of raising a child Jewishly by myself. Although I had many mixed feelings toward traditional Judaism, there still was never any doubt in my mind that our children would be raised as Jews. "I can't finish what Hitler started," I told my husband before we were married. He agreed to having Jewish children. However, what that meant and how it was to be done was unclear to either of us then.

The words that I heard at lunch that day from my feminist acquaintance were echoed three years later by a conservative male in a mainstream Jewish weekly:

> It is taken for granted that children of intermarriages in which neither partner has converted out of their religion by birth will not be socialized as Jews . . . Their children will definitely be lost to Jewry. (Smolar, 1983)

By that time I had developed a certain ability to respond. I replied in a letter to the editor as follows:

> . . . A self-fulfilling prophesy? When intermarried Jewish parents have to struggle with a Jewish community that has written them and their children off, then, of course the parents' tasks of socializing their children as Jews will be very difficult. Such negativity must certainly turn many intermarried Jews away from Jewish life and is bound to create resentment in those intermarried Jews and their children who are earnestly turning toward Judaism. The problem is as much the Jewish community's as it is the intermarried couples'. The Jewish community must change its attitude — it must become tolerant and welcome intermarried Jews and their families into Jewish life. (Sheldon, 1983)

Another incident happened when our elder daughter was about three years old. I was at a playground one afternoon, standing next to a woman I had known from a havurah, an informal Jewish study and social group that my husband and I were part of. When our first child was born, I wrote a naming ceremony to officially welcome her into the Jewish community with a Jewish name. Traditionally, Jewish boys have an obligatory ritual circumcision ceremony shortly after birth. Girls can have a naming during the synagogue service, although the mother and daughter are often not present. Our naming ceremony was a way to communally honor and celebrate the birth of a Jewish girl. Since we were away from family, the havurah was the community which participated with us in this ceremony. The woman from the havurah, who had spoken the prayers of our newborn daughter's naming ceremony three years earlier, was now watching her at play. Apparently she was noticing her blondeness. She remarked, "I am just trying to decide if she looks Jewish." Once more I reacted with shock and hurt. I thought, but couldn't say, "Of course my daughter IS Jewish." As this woman knew, in Orthodox Jewish law (again) a child is considered to be Jewish simply by having a Jewish birth mother. I remained shaken by her comment for a long time. If I couldn't count on support from a Jew who had participated in our child's naming ceremony, I wondered where I could find it after all? The woman apparently had an image of what a Jewish child should look like, which didn't include being blonde, despite the fact that there have been Jewish children throughout the ages that do not match the dark-haired stereotype. Besides, I didn't think that our daughter should be defined as a Jew on the basis of her appearance, and I didn't expect that another feminist would either. She may not have intended to be hurtful. But I wished that she had been sensitive to the rejecting message that such a statement conveys to an intermarried Jew.

Her remarks were actually very predictable. They reflect traditional Jewish beliefs: the taboo on intermarriage, the fear of assimilation, the need to patrol the borders of what is Jewish and what isn't, continually enforcing and defining those borders, deciding who is in and who is out. I didn't want to be seen as being outside of the borders, even though I had been told that I "officially" was. I couldn't bear to think that the daughter we loved so much was perceived by the Jewish community as tainted. It was an echo of the message I had heard from the Orthodox rabbi, who said that he could not bless our marriage unless my husband converted. I felt so burdened by trying to find my way as a Jew. It was crushing to hear a Jew's doubt—a feminist Jew's doubt—about our child's Jewishness.

I felt that I didn't deserve such remarks. I felt reproached and put in the position of having to prove myself to other Jews who appeared more okay than I because they weren't intermarried. I felt I was being held to a standard that many other Jews, behind the facade of a marriage with a Jewish partner, do not themselves measure up to, for example, Jews who observe kosher dietary practices at home but not outside of the home, Jews who don't keep kosher at all, Jews who work on the sabbath, and so on. These Jews can escape criticism by the Jewish community because Judaism has evolved into official branches that allow a variety of practices. What is not recognized is that an intermarried Jew may or may not be a more observant and caring Jew and a better human being than a nonintermarried Jew. Intermarried Jews are struggling over the same issues that other Jews struggle with. Whether or not we are considered as being central to the Jewish community, we are like other Jews in many ways.

The sense of being an outsider to the larger Jewish community because they are in an intermarriage can be intensified for women who do not feel at home in traditional, male-centered Judaism. For the Jewish woman who wants to fully participate in the synagogue service or administration, who wants to express her spirituality and affiliation through the synagogue, there are the usual misogynist impediments that face women in all organized religions. The rejection of intermarried Jewish women by Judaism is echoed by the rejection of feminist women generally in Judaism, and echoed by the resistance of organized religion to change. Thus, the opposition is compounded in the case of the intermarried Jewish *woman*.

I can well describe the feeling of being a woman outsider in my own religion by relating the following incident. When our firstborn was three or four years old, I started going to Friday evening services with her. The synagogue was a long drive from our house and the service came at the end of a tiring week, but I felt fairly comfortable and reflective there. I wanted to celebrate the sabbath service. I loved hearing the woman cantor sing, and one of the rabbis was a woman.

The service was held in a space that was filled with energy for me. One evening, when the service was over, and all of the congregation had adjourned to have refreshments in another room, my preschooler dragged me back to this room. I pulled open the heavy wooden doors and entered. We were alone in the large energy-filled space. She ran down the center aisle and up the steps to the bima (pulpit). I followed her saying, "No, you can't go up there!" I went up to bring her down and out of the room. I stood on the bima, in front of the place where the Torah (Old Testament) is kept and beneath the Eternal Light, a lamp that burns continually. I was trembling with emotion and started to cry. I realized that I was standing in a place where I felt I didn't belong. I didn't have the right to be there. My daughter, on the other hand, had run up here with great glee. There was no doubt in her mind that she belonged here. I took this all in, lingered a while, and then we left. Why did I feel I didn't belong there? At the time I thought it was my sense of being an outsider Jew because I was a woman. I see now how this also reflects the negativism toward intermarriage that I had experienced and must have internalized.

The complex web of feelings of an intermarried Jew is also compounded by a Jew's own fear of annihilation. I remember sitting in a movie theater in Manhattan when I was about 16 years old, in the late 1950's. I was watching Alain Resnais' film "Night and Fog." It was in color, but it moved dramatically into black and white for scenes of the concentration camps. Although I had been hearing and reading about the camps at that time, I hadn't seen the horrors so graphically. It was overwhelming. I sat alone, frozen in the dark, realizing how vulnerable I and my family and friends were just because we were Jews. My Jewish world, that I had associated with warmth and security and home, was suddenly different. And I was utterly terrified.

In my own odyssey, I am feeling much less rejection by Jews these days and I attribute it to a few things. I have become a bit clearer about my relationship to Judaism. Some of my bitterness and hurt at being considered an outsider just because I am a woman is gone. I am finding other Jewish feminists with whom I can have a meaningful spiritual connection. With some of them I am creating meaningful new rituals (Katz, Sheldon & Siegel, 1990; Katz, Sheldon & Siegel, in press). In this way, the shape of a feminist religious expression is becoming clearer. That is to say, the shape of a much longed for Judaism in which I feel included is slowly forming. My husband still supports my efforts to find meaningful spirituality. One year we spent a Passover seder as guests of another family. The traditional seder was controlled by the Jewish patriarch. The woman's role was to cook the immense meal and do the social planning for the event. It was difficult to voice a woman's point of view that evening. The next night, in our own home, our elder daughter led us in our own seder. It has become a tradition in our home to set a cup of wine and open the door not only for the prophet Elijah (which is part of the traditional seder), but also for Miriam, the woman who found baby Moses in the bull rushes. This year we will add a song about how the Jewish midwives, Shifra and Puah, foiled Pharaoh's attempt to kill Jewish children. In religious ritual led by a feminist, there is more room for a woman's voice, and for innovation and collaboration by other family members.

Our two daughters, now seven and ten years old, are students in a somewhat progressive Talmud Torah day school. At school they have tefillah (morning prayers and singing) every day. They are developing synagogue skills, and learning Hebrew and Torah. They are getting a nonsuperficial Jewish education. They are living in a community of Jewish friends and celebrating Jewish holidays as a matter of course. I know that I could not raise them Jewishly without the help that such a community provides.

There are many other children of religiously mixed marriages at their school. So I know that in this community, Judaism is functioning with the reality of intermarriage. I hope that these intermarried Jews will continue to have an effect on the form of this community. I know that my daughters are part of a Jewish community in which they feel comfortable. We have not figured out all of the difficulties of living in the modern world, not the least of which is being a family with two parents who have different religions.

This year, our elder daughter is in the fourth grade at Talmud Torah. She is studying Torah to be able to read it in the original biblical Hebrew. It is my nonJewish husband, who knows no Hebrew, who takes the initiative and has the patience to help her with her Hebrew night after night. He and our daughter sit nestled together in a big easy chair. He holds her Hebrew flash cards up one by one. She reads them and translates. He corrects her if necessary. The answer is on the back of the card. He gives her tricks to remember the difficult words. He praises her for good work. Is this just another weary father helping his daughter with her school work at the end of a long day? I smile. Our daughter is doing well in Hebrew and Torah.

Just a few weeks ago I was listening to a radio program that reported on a conference which was held to explain why Scandinavians were better able to resist the Holocaust and save Jews (Cooperman, 1989). The reason given was intermarriage. As it turns out, intermarriage was fairly common in countries like Denmark, where nonJews had a history of tolerance toward Jews. This led the Danish people to collectively obstruct German attempts to kill Jews. In other words, intermarriage saved many Jews in Scandinavia during the Holocaust. When I heard this, I smiled and savored the irony.

What are the implications of my story for those who counsel Jewish women who are in or contemplating intermarriage? Such a woman will enter a borderland which is shaped in a complex way by traditional Jewish culture as well as her own personal history. Women will differ in the degree to which developing a Jewish spirituality matters. They may see their connection to Judaism as a purely cultural rather than spiritual one, and this may change over their lifetime. The male-focused core of Judaism is resistant to change and exerts a powerful influence on our imaginations and sense of what is possible. Being a member of a minority religion in a Christian country adds to the stress. If a couple has children, there are many decisions around the children that will be affected by the fact of intermarriage. But I choose not to lose sight of the fact that intermarriage is also an opportunity to create meaningful and symbolically creative acts of community and spirituality. The complexities of such a state of being, with its possibilities and costs, are captured so well for me by the words of Gloria Anzaldúa (Moraga and Anzaldúa, 1983), who lives in her own borderland as a Chicana, Tejana, Lesbian, working class, writer: "Who me confused? Ambivalent? Not so. Only your labels split me."

REFERENCES

Cooperman, D. (1989). Comments made on Take Out, Minneapolis: KUOM-Radio, November.

Hillel. *Mishnah Avot* 1:14. In R. Travers Herford (1962), *The ethics of the Talmud* (pp. 33-34). New York: Schocken Books.

Katz, N., Sheldon, A., & Siegel, R. J. (1990). Hanukah: Lighting the way to women's empowerment. In *Bridges*, Vol. 1(2)

Katz, N., Sheldon, A., & Siegel, R. J. (In Press). Hanukah: A feminist cere-mony. Women's Institute for Continuing Jewish Education. San Diego, CA.

Moraga, C., & Anzaldúa, G. (1983). *This bridge called my back: Writings by radical women of color*. New York: Kitchen Table/Women of Color Press.

Sheldon, A. (1983, October 28). Letter to the Editor, *The New York Jewish Week*, p. 21.

Smolar, B. (1983, September 23). Article written for the *The New York Jewish Week*.

Midlife Transitions Among Jewish Women: Counseling Issues

Rachel Aber Schlesinger

In learning to speak our experience and situation we insist on the right to begin where we are, to stand as subjects of our sentences, and to hear one another as the authoritative speakers of our own experiences. (Smith, 1975, p. 2)

In 1983 I was a doctoral student. I had recently made a major change in my life, re-entering university 20 years after my last degree. With thoughts of process, transitions, roles of Jewish women, and an investigation of supports, I conducted in-depth interviews with 22 Jewish women, between the ages of 45 and 65 (Schlesinger, 1983). One purpose of this investigation was to see how women understood changes in their lives, and my focus was re-entry into the paid work force after having been at home for at least ten years. Over the years I kept in contact with the women, noting additional changes in their lives. They helped form my ideas of how transitions are experienced and understood. We often talk about change, acknowledging that it can be painful, yet it leads to growth and maturity and the ability to make new beginnings throughout our longer life span. As a woman, working with other women, I felt the need to understand this change process.

Rachel Aber Schlesinger is an assistant professor, Division of Social Science, York University, Toronto, Ontario, Canada, and is a member of NWA, a feminist consulting group in Toronto.

METHODOLOGY

The therapist listens, and allows the voice of the client to be heard. As I conducted interviews, only the voice of the respondent was heard, yet it is clear that each interview was in itself an intervention. Each woman was interviewed several times over the course of two years. The interviews were recorded on audio tapes, transcribed, and then brought back to the woman for further clarification, using a grounded theory methodology. Talking about the change of leaving the private world to enter the public one allowed women to think about process, evaluate decisions, and articulate what supports they felt were missing.

OBJECTIVES

There were several concepts I wished to explore. One issue was to examine how being Jewish affected the decisions that these 22 women made about returning to paid work. In the early 1980's, going to work represented a major transition for this group of middle aged, middle class Jewish women living in Toronto, Canada. A second related issue was to discover how women perceived and understood changes or transitions. Did they view change as a process, and if so, were there any stages they could identify? Did they feel that this transition could lead to a changed concept of self? Finally, I wanted to learn where women found support, or recognized the lack of support, as they moved through the transition from home to paid work.

FINDINGS:
PERCEPTIONS OF CHANGE, AND BEING JEWISH

A decade ago Jewish women who entered the work force while their friends remained at home felt vulnerable, isolated and guilty. Many factors accounted for these feelings. Women faced a great deal of opposition from husbands, children, in-laws, friends, and total strangers, who all felt free to criticize them. Even the media bombarded them with images of women caring for home and hearth, directing them to buy products for their own beauty and the beautification of the home.

The Jewish community of Toronto, with voices raised in synagogues, volunteer organizations and Hebrew day schools, stressed that women provided the vital link from one generation to the other. It was their responsibility to maintain the tradition that ensures continuity of Jewish identity of family members. This is the ascribed role of the Jewish woman. As women shared their perceptions of a change process, they identified ways their concepts of what it meant to be a Jewish women changed as well. In coping with the strains, role shifts, and role discontinuity of working outside the home, more than half of the women redefined their Jewish agenda.

Most of these women identified stages in the change process. The following model, that I developed as part of a larger study (Schlesinger, 1983), emerged from the content of the interviews. The process was seen as a typical problem solving paradigm that can be summed up in a *R E A L* model: stages of Reality, Explorations, Action and Learning.

1. Reality

The first stage involved a changing reality. It was difficult for the respondents to identify a specific event or point to a time that prompted the decision to go into the paid work force. As these Jewish women were growing up there was no question of remaining single. Moreover, marriage was seen as an end in itself, the reaching of a goal, not as a beginning. The reality, however, found many women unprepared. Ora expresses her ambivalence:

> Getting married, to me, was like a little death. I didn't know what hit me. I was already an old maid at 23. I was a social worker, and I knew that I could never work again. It wasn't done . . . I don't know where I got the idea that everything has to stop at marriage . . . but there was no other model for me, no one to tell me. I remember a feeling of mourning at my marriage. I didn't want to lose my name, and I didn't want to lose myself.

Ora admitted that she had no real concept of what being married meant beyond the stereotypic role of the Jewish wife and mother.

The women who were interviewed spent the early years of marriage having from two to five children, cooking, preparing for the Jewish holidays, volunteering in the Jewish community, and often helping husbands establish themselves. Although many worked in family businesses none felt she had worked, since work was defined as something that was outside family responsibilities, and was paid. The first stage in the re-entry process was characterized by a period of dissatisfaction that led to a process of reflection and an attempt to understand why the dream wasn't the reality.

2. Explorations

The second stage was one of explorations, and led to looking for alternatives. The following factors were identified: boredom, feelings of uselessness, low self esteem and even lower perceived status, isolation, a desire to use skills, and a need on the part of some to prepare to be independent. This period lasted from two to five years. It was difficult to move away from the respected role of the Jewish mother, wife and community worker. This stage included exploring options, evaluating their own skills and abilities, and a sense of drifting rather than making decisions. Finally, for some women, the feeling of isolation and loneliness gave way to seeing themselves as pioneers.

> I'll never forget that nobody in their right mind went to work
> . . . Friends wanted to know everything. Did it mean that my
> marriage was breaking up? How did I do it? What did I do the
> first thing in the morning? They had loads of questions. I'll
> never forget that they cried; I guess they were thinking of
> themselves. I was early. (Fran)

There were pushes into the paid work force, but there were also factors pulling them back into the home. These included doubts about their abilities, lack of training, few job opportunities, difficulty in decision making, need to tend to family members, and finally, guilt, and anger. It was not clear to the women at whom the anger was directed—at self or others. These women had volunteered for this study, and had identified themselves as Jewish women, concerned with their Jewish identity. This same identity made it difficult to move out of the home for long hours each day. They felt guilty if they were not home for the children, and if they did not cook meals from scratch (June's comment). In entering the workforce, it seemed as if they were putting their own needs ahead of those of their family members. How would the children get to Hebrew school, to Bar and Bat Mitzvah lessons if they were not there to take them? The respondents were good at running their homes. They received rewards for this. They were praised, not in terms of the woman of valor of the Psalms, but in the feedback that they got for taking care of others. The Sabbath candles were lit on time, the festive table was set. Positive feedback came when women did what was expected, and status was attained not only in the family, but in the positions they held in Zionist and synagogue groups. As they moved into the work force, they felt they would be asked to give up those aspects of their lives for which they received praise. In return, they would move with uncertainty into a public world, where they had to compete on different levels, and often with younger women.

They were angry, and the anger was directed at themselves, and their assumptions that there was only one way to be a good Jewish wife and mother, and that was to serve others. At this point, however, four women thought the price was too high. They took jobs, but left them because they could not continue to work without giving up their "Jewishness" in observance or belief. They were all over fifty-five years of age, and felt that paid work would bring short-term satisfactions, but the price was too great. Relationships were more important, and they felt they could not maintain these and work at the same time.

It was remarkable that all of these women felt they had received mixed messages from their own mothers about fulfilling the role of the Jewish woman. They valued these roles and traditions, and were reluctant to give them up. The clash arose between doing what was taught and valued by myth and family traditions versus their own reality. There is a fine line between resentment of the Jewish woman's ascribed role and the rejection of her role. The respondents walked the line of compromise.

Sara mentioned that every Jewish holiday, and especially Pass-over, reminded her that "priorities are in celebrating the holidays, and there isn't much energy for anything else." Janet found that fighting the demands of others was not possible for her: "I wouldn't commit myself to a strong goal, because it would mean fighting . . . that wasn't my style." Fran was angry not at her family, but for the lack of support she received from Jewish community agencies. "Jewish women are not supposed to go to work, that's the official line, so forget any kind of help that might come in the form of day care or support groups."

3. Action

The next stage was that of action. Since all the women were working, this step had already been taken. The time period, how-ever, varies for each woman. The younger women, aged 40-45, took less than 2 years; the older women, aged 46-65, took longer. They felt that the process took from three to ten years, from think-ing about work, to actually getting a job. This step involved making a public commitment to change. They told others about it. They had to deal with juggling timetables, with fears of being too old for the job, and with uncertainty once again. They had to make cutbacks, giving up responsibility in the organized Jewish community, learn-ing how to say "no" — to children, to parents, to husbands, and to friends in Hadassah and other Jewish women's service organiza-tions.

A changing sense of personal identity emerged from the inter-views. Women reported a sense of rediscovery at this stage, and found aspects of themselves they had not acknowledged for many years.

> I really felt reluctant about taking the job. I worried how I was going to do it, how I was going to get to the office, even where I was going to park. Everything was a problem . . . On the first day the phone rang in my office, and when I answered, there was my old voice, the one I had lost years ago, the one I had forgotten. There was the old, competent me; I found myself again. (Sara)

4. Learning

The final stage was one of evaluation. For some women this was indeed a recognition of thinking about themselves in new ways. In this period they tested their new image of self, they spoke about how they understood a sense of control over their own lives, and the meaning of work — in terms of money earned, skills learned, self-respect, and decision making.

The women who traveled furthest in the journey toward a new sense of self were the more observant women interviewed for this research. Marcie saw herself as "shedding an old skin." Her understanding of her religious role, for example, underwent profound shifts.

> I am only realizing now that we are all wearing our own hand-cuffs. I didn't realize before that I also have the keys. We impose our own prison walls. I only realized this recently, preparing for Passover. I was put into bondage . . . one day I said I couldn't take it any longer. Boy was that a revelation. First of all that I could say it, and then that others listened. I forgot there were options; now I exercise them.

Marcie gave herself permission to relinquish part of the previously valued Jewish role. Yet she retained a portion of her volunteer commitments, felt that Jewish education for her children was vital, and was not willing to give up the meaning (even if part of the form changed) of religious traditions. The Sabbath and holiday observances were important, ritualized not only in religious terms, but to foster family togetherness. Sabbath dinners were the times set aside to pick up the pieces lost during the busy week. Virtually each woman mentioned the Sabbath, finding in this institutionalized day of rest a valuable resource.

The Toronto Jewish community has been slow to acknowledge the changing role of the Jewish woman. There is a network of synagogues, community centers, schools and volunteer organizations that service the 130,000 affiliated Jews. This is a traditional community, with a large majority being first generation settlers (Schlesinger, 1987). There is a need for counseling and for putting women in contact with each other. There is also ideological support that

should be given. Women need to feel their expanded roles are valued and valid, in the home, in their relationships, and in the context
of their religious and secular lives. Many complained they had no
one to talk with.

> It is really sad that women can't talk to each other. We would
> have helped each other, but we didn't know how. We had to
> struggle alone. (Leah)

The image of the helpmate, Eve, is at variance with the "equal"
mate, Lilith.

IMPLICATIONS FOR FEMINIST THERAPY

These women fought against religious and cultural attitudes and
norms to change their lives. Initially, many sensed a feeling of loss.
They had left behind the familiar role, a stage of certainty, to enter a
stage of disequilibrium and uncertainty. Together with this loss was
a feeling of being alone, of isolation, and a sense of guilt. On many
levels help was needed, but rarely available. They were dealing
with role discontinuity, with the changes in the role of the Jewish
woman, and with the real difficulties encountered in entering the
paid work force at a later age and with less work experience than
younger workers.

Help was sought and women found each other. I introduced some
of these women to one another after the formal part of this research
was over. A few began to meet on a regular basis and even now,
seven years later, six of the women are still together as a support
group.

The issue of guilt was discussed. The group felt that they had
neglected some aspect of their lives, be it children, mates, elderly
parents, even friends and community responsibilities. Some women
worked out issues with the help of counseling. Their experiences
help to understand ways that professionals can guide women
through the change process. Feminist therapists have unique in-
sights into helping women make transitions. We bring a critical
analysis of the conditions of women in a patriarchal society, such as
Judaism, and the society at large. We hold as central the idea that

we derive knowledge from each other and that it connects to and grows out of our own daily experiences.

Counseling is seen as many things, from an educational process to a healing process, and indeed a political process. As a feminist I am rooted in my own life experiences, and these include my family *and* my religion. Therapists can play a vital role in transitions. For example:

1. Both therapists and clients need to acknowledge that change is indeed a process. Perhaps a client will have to halt at a particular stage, at least for a period of time. For some, knowing that you can take small steps is also important. Many of the women in this study took years to understand the change process. It would be a mistake to think that women can be hurried through these stages, or that they can arrive at a transition quicker, and with less pain. Transitions are not quickies, and they can only be understood at the pace of the individual woman. She needs time and help to deal with the various systems that affect her life. As this study indicated, the change impacted on her relationships, her responsibilities and her sense of roles.

2. As a therapist I need to be aware of the social, cultural and religious background of the client. Religious values and beliefs impinge on transitions. The greater the degree of affiliation with one's culture, religion, and ethnic background, the more difficult it was for the women to move in directions that would place them in conflict with these values. Value-laden areas, like religious beliefs, are resistant to change. Women felt they understood themselves when they began to make choices about Jewish roles and rules.

3. The ability to change is related to family status. The women in this study felt that they had "invested" in their relationships, and now wanted some help in return. Within a few years of this study, many relationships changed. Two women left long-term partners, one divorced, three became widows, and four "retired" from their jobs to spend time with aging parents, ailing husbands, or children and grandchildren.

4. Women give support to each other. We need to feel good about sharing our experiences, our successes and our failures. Communication is a vital way to break the feeling of isolation.

5. Some women will react well to *bibliotherapy*. Over the years

women have begun to find a voice, and have spoken and written about issues that relate to change. Reading, and then discussing the written experiences, are valuable tools for some of us.

6. Peer counseling, both on the job and during the process of making a change, is important. We need mentors and models. Women have a right to ask for help. They must not feel that it is somehow a failing to ask for guidance and support in making a major change.

REFERENCES

Schlesinger, R. (1983). Jewish women in transition, Unpublished doctoral thesis, University of Toronto.

Schlesinger, R. (1987). In R. Palomba & L. Schamgar-Handelmann (Eds.), *Alternative patterns of family life in modern societies* (pp. 227-242). Rome, Italy: IRP.

Smith, D., & David, S. (1975). *Women look at psychiatry*, Vancouver: Press Gang Publications.

All in the Family:
Violence in the Jewish Home

Betsy Giller

The family is one of the basic units of society and insures the perpetuation of culture and transmission of values and mores. Within each culture an idealized conception of the family has evolved. The contrast between these ideals of what should be and the realities of what actually exists in family life is an ongoing source of tension in both the American Jewish family as well as other American families. Family violence is affected by this tension. It exists in each ethnic and religious community, where it is also excluded in specific ways from the framework of acceptable family behavior.

The Jew in American society functions with three sets of conflicting standards regarding the family, each of which contribute to the existence of Jewish family violence and to the difficulty in acknowledging that such violence exists. First, there is the value system of the idealized American family, assumed to be Christian, white and middle class, in contrast to the realities of daily American family life. Second, there is the discrepancy between the Jewish value system and what actually occurs within the Jewish family. Third, there is the tension between how Jews want non-Jews to view them and the reality of life in Jewish families and in the Jewish community. Jewish women, furthermore, are affected both by

Betsy Giller, LCSW, MAJCS, is currently an Emergency Service therapist at Northwest Center for Community Mental Health in Reston, VA. She is past coordinator and founder of the Family Violence Project of Jewish Family Service of Los Angeles. The author wishes to acknowledge the assistance of Ellen Goldsmith, LCSW, Ellen Ledley, LCSW, and Rabbi Julie Spitzer in the preparation of this article.

American gender roles and Jewish stereotypic expectations for women.

The myths about the American family are well reflected in the popular American culture. The best known example of this ideal is the "Father Knows Best" family, where everyone loves one another, listens warmly and caringly to one another. Most importantly, no serious conflict ever arises. This is in stark contrast to the turmoil and travail of present day life. This myth is what Straus and Steinmetz (1974) refer to as "the myth of family consensus and harmony," which encourages the view that family violence is nonnormative and deviant, and therefore can be disregarded as being a major societal problem.

The Jewish tradition is also replete with notions of harmony and love between family members. The rabbinic conception of marriage as an expression of holiness or "kiddushin," demonstrates the high level of expectation that the marital couple must contend with. In reality, however, marriage is fraught with tension which the couple must resolve peacefully, within the sometimes ambiguous boundaries of Jewish tradition.

Jewish values regarding marriage and child-rearing are most succinctly expressed in the terms "shalom bayit" or "peace in the home." Violation of these idealized "shoulds" has such stigma attached to it that reaching out for help to treat problems such as family violence is rarely even considered within the Jewish community. The desire not to challenge the myth of the Jewish family's immunity to such problems leads family members to deny what goes on in their families. They continue to deny the abusive behavior even when they recognize the acts as being harmful or even dangerous. Most families, therefore, do not seek help, while the few who do are often ignored because of the community's need to maintain its idealized vision of the Jewish family.

The phrase, "A shanda for the Goyim" or "It's a shame for the non-Jews to know" expresses the third tension. It is difficult for Jews to acknowledge serious problems, such as family violence, and to seek help in solving them outside the Jewish community. Many Jews would like to believe that Jewish families are different from other families. There is shame in acknowledging to ourselves or to non-Jews that we may suffer from the same problems and may need help. All three of these tensions can be implicated in explaining why it has been so difficult to acknowledge the existence of family violence in the Jewish community, and to provide help for those involved in this problem.

Women also operate with culturally determined stereotypic expectations, which normalize certain behaviors and exclude others. Jewish tradition conveys very specific and powerful messages about caregiving as the only acceptable role for Jewish women. When women see their primary role as emotional caretakers in the family, they can become immobilized in the face of violence in their own families. This can lead to an overwhelming sense of guilt, responsibility, and a sense of failure in their primary roles. The ensuing feeling of shame leads to isolation, preventing the admission of such abject failure, and allowing the continuation of the violence.

Jewish women operate under an additional set of stereotypes which further functions to suppress them and prevent them from extricating themselves from violent situations. Jewish women have been portrayed as extremely powerful within the home, as controlling and verbally domineering, provoking otherwise docile men to lash out. On the other hand, Jewish women have been described as "Jewish American Princesses," passive, dependent, whiny and entitled, also provocative to their partners. This stereotype was even used as a defense in a murder trial of a man who killed his wife, but was acquitted due to his wife's extreme provocation and "JAP demands" leading to his temporary insanity (Frondorf, 1988). In such cases, the partners are seen as victims while the women are seen as victimizers.

STATISTICS

What are the realities of Jewish family violence in general and wife battering in particular? In 1980, a study of Jewish family violence was conducted under the auspices of Hebrew Union College and University of Southern California (Giller & Goldsmith, 1980), surveying active members of a number of Los Angeles synagogues. The findings are alarming.

In spite of the silence usually surrounding Jewish family violence, and contrary to expectations, a great deal of information regarding Jewish family violence was exposed by each group contacted.

All professionals who participated in the study knew of cases of Jewish family violence. Almost all of the rabbis interviewed reported some knowledge of the problem. The congregants revealed a great deal of information regarding family violence. Every synagogue produced cases of family violence.

From 209 respondents, a total of 22 spousal abuse and 118 child abuse cases were revealed. Four cases of sexual abuse and 11 cases of social isolation were also reported.

There were 129 incidents of siblings striking one another. The abuse ranged from sibling squabbles to an incident of an older brother pushing his younger brother out of a moving car.

These findings are consistent with all of the general literature surveyed (Finkelhor, Gelles, Hotaling & Straus, 1983). Although Jews were under-represented in earlier studies, these findings indicate that the high level of violence which exists in the general community also occurs in the Jewish community. This incorporates the entire range of family violence, including sibling violence, spousal abuse, and child abuse.

The findings also indicate that violence is not a phenomenon confined to any one segment of the Jewish community. No difference was found in the amount of violence reported by reform, orthodox or conservative Jews. With one exception, none of the other demographic data revealed any differences between those who were involved in the violence, and those who were not. These variables include gender, level of education, marital status, and country of origin of the family. This is consistent with all of the family violence literature which states that violence exists across all social boundaries. It is interesting to note that the only demographic information which showed a difference was income. In contrast to the myth that violence is a phenomenon of the lower socio-economic class, it was found that those respondents with higher incomes were more likely to be involved with intrafamilial violence.

Repeatedly in the literature, family violence has been shown to be a phenomenon transmitted from generation to generation (Gelles, 1974). Child abusers were often abused children and wife batterers were often both abused children and witnesses to the battering of their mothers by their fathers. This was strongly validated by findings in this study. When violence done to the respondent was correlated with violence done by him or her, a very high association was shown. Second, when violence done by the respondent was correlated with violence done by other family members to one another, an equally high association emerged. These two findings strongly indicate that Jews, like non-Jews, transmit family violence from one generation to the next. Additionally, the psychosocial stressors that impact a family also have a powerful impact on the generational transmission of family violence. Violent oppression of Jews, such as the experience of pogroms in Europe, the immigrant experience in the early 1900's in America and most powerfully, the experience of survivors of the Holocaust and their families serve to generate rage and model violent means of interaction which find expression within the family. The family is not, therefore, the seat of harmony and "shalom bayit" that traditional values indicate it should be. Instead it may be a training ground for the perpetuation of further violence in the home.

As a direct result of this study, Jewish Family Service of Los Angeles initiated The Family Violence Project, a program to reach out to and treat Jews involved with Jewish family violence. Over the six years of its existence, the project has delivered services to over 650 violent families, most of whom are Jewish, who run the gamut from Orthodox to unaffiliated, poverty level to extremely high socio-economic status, American born and immigrants, validating the above findings.

CLINICAL IMPLICATIONS

As therapists, we are not immune to the myths and stereotypes discussed above. Before we can begin any clinical intervention, we must examine and counteract the distortions of our perceptions and judgement which these filters cause. Victims of violence in general are often invisible when they do not fit the usual stereotypes. Unless we can remove our blindspots, we run the risk of not recognizing domestic violence when it affects women who are not of color, are not of lower socio-economic means, who might be educated or in fact might be Jewish.

As clinicians, we must challenge our own internalized stereo-types in order to ask the questions necessary to allow women and families cowed by shame to admit to the violence, trauma and danger with which they live. We must examine our view of Jewish men in order not to miss the possibility that the scholar, doctor or lawyer may also be violent or sexually abusive, and that the professional Jewish woman may also be a victim of domestic violence. We also must look at other segments of the Jewish community as vulnerable: the elderly, the Israeli, Russian or other immigrant communities.

Once these obstacles between therapist and client are reduced, the therapist is better able to examine each client's situation clearly and to plan and implement interventions which truly fit her/his circumstances.

Interventions with Jewish battered women must first and fore-most address issues of physical safety for the woman and her children. The Jewish components of the problem must also be addressed. These will vary depending upon the woman's family background, her current affiliation, degree of ethnic and religious identification and that of her partner. This component is obviously relevant for women who are currently observant or are from religious backgrounds, but the Jewish component of a client's identity may be an equally powerful force regardless of affiliation or current practice. Note that the absence of Jewish identification or isolation from the Jewish community can be both a result of the abuse or part of what perpetuates it. Clients who have strong ties within the community may still feel isolated in that they feel constrained from revealing the violence to those within the community. They are further isolated due to their sense of shame and guilt encouraged by gender-role expectations within Judaism. These pressures are part of what keeps Jewish women from being able to take action on their own behalf. Crisis intervention is almost always necessary during the course of treatment due to the cyclical nature of family violence. The use of individual therapy, both supportive and psychodynami-cally-oriented is also indicated (Fleming, 1979; Walker, 1984; Wo-darski, 1987).

In addition, groups for women have been shown to be vital in the empowering process that allows women to make the investment in themselves that will enable them to decrease feelings of helplessness and powerlessness, to improve self-esteem, to alter their circumstances and free themselves from violent relationships (Ball, 1977; NiCarthy, 1984). Groups that include other Jewish women can help clients to lessen the shame, isolation and stigma induced by those societal stereotypes which make Jewish abused women invisible, even to themselves.

Services for abusers and children must also be provided. Groups are especially effective with abusive men, to break down the powerful denial that is supported by cultural ideas about violence (Ganley, 1985). Having a partner in a Jewish abusive men's group can be liberating for women as well. One client stated "my husband isn't Jewish when he is violent." Knowing of a group of Jewish abusive men allowed this woman to accept herself and her partner as Jewish, and also as being abused and abusive.

Initial interventions with abusive men must be behavioral, focusing on the identification of violence and on the thoughts and physical sensations which precede violent outbursts, in order to limit further abuse by developing controls. Further interventions include helping men to identify and verbalize feelings in order to minimize acting them out. Supportive treatment focused on assertiveness training and increasing self-esteem is also indicated.

Services to children of abused women should be included, making the therapist available to validate the children's experience, and to help them label it. Family interventions can be useful, especially if a woman has separated from an abusive partner. Role modeling of non-violent, non-abusive conflict resolution is vital in the family healing process. Groups are also powerful tools for children to lessen their shame, isolation and sense of responsibility for the family situation.

Couples' therapy is not indicated, until each partner has been in group treatment and controls have been put in place to allow for protection from violence. Issues of gender-role expectations and power balance are often part of conjoint treatment once the couple is ready. Communication problems must also be addressed, as well as issues stemming from families of origin, especially if they were violent or abusive.

Using a client's cultural context can strengthen an intervention and use the client's own frame of references to solidify gains and draw upon existing strengths. Within the Jewish tradition, there are strong female role models with whom to identify as well as an extensive rich history of confronting and overcoming oppression which can be utilized as imagery in treatment with battered women. The Family Violence Project of Los Angeles, for example, uses the Passover Seder* as a vehicle for abused women to creatively explore themes of violence, oppression and redemption within a Jewish context. The holiday of Sukkot,** and the image of "Sukkat Shalom" or a "shelter of peace" has been used as a forum from rabbinical pulpits to educate the Jewish community about Jewish family violence. Additionally, it is important to note that there are rabbinic commentaries and responsa*** which directly prohibit wife battering, and use this as the basis for granting a woman a get.**** This information can be liberating to traditional Jewish women who are in violent homes (Agus, 1979; Spitzer, 1985).

CONCLUSION

The existence of Jewish family violence and of Jewish battered women has long been hidden. For the past 10 years, a growing body of experience and research has exposed and documented the magnitude of the problem.

It is now time to allow those who suffer under the pain and oppression of violence to come forward, to heal and be healed. As therapists, by challenging our own deeply held beliefs, we can begin the healing process and enable movement from pain and oppression to strength and empowerment. We can empower our clients by using sound clinical judgement, within the client's cultural and spiritual context.

Jewish family violence will continue as long as institutions both

---

*Ritual celebration of the holiday of Passover, commemorating the liberation of Jews from slavery in Egypt.

**Jewish harvest festival, celebrated using a temporary shelter or sukkah.

*** Body of Rabbinic responses to petitions or questions, part of Jewish Rabbinic law.

****Jewish religious divorce decree, necessary for religious remarriage, granted only by husband.

within and beyond the Jewish community perpetuate myths about women, Jewish women and Jewish families. Those who have experience with the impact of violence, both as its victims, and as those who serve those victims, are obligated to strive for change. Healing must include change on a community and societal scale. Healing must involve education, the breaking down of stereotyping, and the commitment of an entire community to the honest recognition and prevention of Jewish family violence.

REFERENCES

Agus, I. (1979). *Rabbi Meir of Rothenburg*, Vol.1. New York: Jewish Theological Seminary.

Ball, M. (1977). Issues of violence in family casework. *Social Casework* 58(1), 13-20.

Finkelhor, D., Gelles, R., Hotaling, G., & Straus, M., (Eds.) (1983). *The dark side of families*. Beverly Hills: Sage Publications.

Fleming, J. (1979). *Stopping wife abuse: A guide to the emotional, psychological, and legal implications for the abused woman and those helping her*. Garden City, New York: Anchor Press/Doubleday.

Frondorf, S. (1988). *Death of a "Jewish American Princess": The true story of a victim on trial*. New York: Villard Books.

Ganley, A. (1985). *Court mandated counseling for men who batter: A three day workshop for mental health professionals*. Washington, DC: Center for Women, Policy Studies.

Gelles, R. (1974). *The violent home*. Beverly Hills: Sage Publications.

Giller, B., & Goldsmith, E. (1980). *All in the family: A study of intra-familial violence in the Los Angeles Jewish community*. Master's Thesis, Hebrew Union College/University of Southern California.

NiCarthy, G. (1984). *Talking it out: A guide to groups for abused women*. Seattle, Washington: Seal Press.

Spitzer, J.R. (1985). *Spousal abuse in rabbinic and contemporary Judaism*. New York: National Federation of Temple Sisterhoods.

Straus, M., & Steinmetz, S. (1974). *Violence in the family*. New York: Harper and Row.

Walker, L. (1984). *The battered woman syndrome*. New York: Springer Publishing Company.

Wodarski, J. (1987). An examination of spouse abuse: Practice issues for the profession. *Clinical Social Work Journal*, 15(2), 172-187.

Cultural Undertones in Therapeutic Work with a Psychotic Jewish Patient

Susan L. Steinberg

Although I have been a Jewish woman psychotherapist for some time, I have only recently become aware that being a Jewish woman has had an effect on my professional work. I feel embarrassed by this realization on three counts. As a psychologist, I expect a level of self-awareness in myself that includes culturally based "issues," especially after having had supervision focused on uncovering countertransference reactions and being in my own in-depth psychotherapy. While cultural concerns were examined in both settings, they were not specifically identified as Jewish identity issues. As a Jewish person, I am committed to understanding what Judaism means in my life, how I define Judaism and how it defines me. As a feminist, I strive to be sensitive to the needs and concerns of minority groups by valuing all aspects of an individual's personality and self-definition, as well as attempting to counteract the devaluation of minority groups that so often occurs in our sexist and ethnocentric society.

Nevertheless, prior to this recent insight, my psychological explorations and my cultural awareness or sensitivity had been kept separate and distinct. More specifically, I hardly ever associated my "personal issues" or "countertransference reactions" with any cultural factors. I saw these "issues" or "reactions" as the results of ingrained idiosyncratic interpersonal patterns that I had learned in

Susan L. Steinberg, PhD, is currently a psychology postdoctoral fellow specializing in inpatient psychiatry at Harbor-UCLA Medical Center in Los Angeles. She received her doctoral degree from Clark University and completed her predoctoral internship at the Veterans' Administration Medical Center in Palo Alto, CA.

111

my family of origin. Thus, I did not assume that my cultural heritage could have clear-cut relevance to my work.

It was during my postdoctoral fellowship that I was struck most profoundly by the seemingly "primitive" and forceful influence of Judaism on my professional work. I was working on an inpatient psychiatry ward for chronic mentally ill patients at a county hospital in Los Angeles. This ward, like all other LA county psychiatric wards, was experiencing full-force the effects of a crumbling mental health system. This translated into sicker patients, both mentally and physically, shorter stays, legal hassles, and low staff to patient ratios. In short, both patients and staff were overwhelmed.

When I arrived on the ward I learned that one of the postdoc's major responsibilities was to lead the group psychotherapy program. Quite anxious about how to attend to the degree and variety of psychopathology and the number of patients in the group, I quickly got out my copy of Yalom's (1983) *Inpatient Group Psychotherapy* and began reading. I realized, rather soon, that much of what he had written wasn't applicable. His "low functioning" groups were considerably higher functioning than our "high functioning" groups. So what next? I talked to the staff who had been running groups (mostly trainees), and found that mostly everyone (staff and patients) avoided going to group. If they went they would grit their teeth and try to get through it some way. Needless to say, I was terrified going into my first group.

"Good morning everyone," I said, "I'm Dr. Steinberg, and this is group therapy." I thought this was an innocuous beginning. I was clearly surprised when a Jewish male patient in his late thirties replied, "Mrs. Steinberg, it's a pleasure to meet you, Shanah Tovah."* I didn't know what to say. I smiled and went on.

As a woman working at a major medical center, I have become desensitized to being called "nurse" or "miss" by patients. I was, however, stunned by the label "Mrs." Immediately, I felt demoted and resentful as I was being lowered from the rank of expert and professional. I also felt apprehensive about being identified as a woman; I didn't want to have to struggle against the expectations/limitations associated with the female role. Somewhat to my sur-

---

*Shanah Tovah — "Happy New Year" (Hebrew expression).

prise, I also felt acknowledged by this funny label. I felt as if this patient had reminded me of some distant relative who would say to me "it is wonderful that you are married and I would like to share with you in the 'nachus'* associated with marriage."

As group continued, this patient, whom I will call Dan, told me he was a Rabbi (a delusion) and talked to me in Yiddish. I had strong and mixed reactions to this. In general, I felt distracted by his comments. I didn't understand Yiddish and couldn't determine if his words had relevance to the group discussion. I also felt ashamed and saddened because I didn't know Yiddish. Dan's discourse brought up images of my elderly grandmother, my last surviving relative to speak fluent Yiddish, and I became acutely aware that she may die soon, leaving the rest of my family cut off from a wealth of Jewish knowledge and tradition. In addition, I felt embarrassed by Dan because he had so quickly identified me as Jewish and responded solely to this part of me. And, I also felt endeared to him, but was not sure how I could use this feeling therapeutically. Would this tenderness be construed as "unprofessional?" Would I be showing favoritism?

As time progressed, I got more comfortable leading group, but I still maintained a distance from Dan in the name of "professional boundaries." After all, he wasn't my individual patient. During this time, Dan became less psychotic and more depressed. He continued to seek me out to *schmooze* in Americanized Yiddish (most of which I understood) and to complain about being on the ward. I mostly smiled, nodded my head empathically, and walked away to talk with my own patients.

Two days prior to Yom Kippur,** Dan came up to me following group to wish me "Good Yontov."*** He told me how sad it was for him to realize he would still be in the hospital on Yom Kippur. He had hoped to have been well enough to be released. Before I had fully registered what he had said, he looked up and asked me if I

---

*nachus—A sense of pleasure and satisfaction that someone you love has done the right thing.

**Yom Kippur—"Day of Atonement." A solemn day of fasting and prayer. The most important day in the Jewish liturgical year.

***Good Yontov—"Happy Holiday" (Yiddish expression).

was going to synagogue or would be with my family for the holiday. Normally when a patient asks me a personal question I *choose* either to answer or not to answer. In this case, I felt I had no choice — it was as if I had received a religious imperative to answer his question. All of a sudden "professionalism" did not matter in the least.

All I could think of was Dan being on the ward on Yom Kippur — the only Jewish patient on the ward — with no public acknowledgement of the importance of this very holy day. There would be no services to go to. Most of the staff would be unaware of the meaning of this holiday. Those who, like Dan, cherished Judaism, would be at their own synagogues or with their own families. Because Dan's psychosis had alienated him from his family, he wouldn't even receive a phone call from a family member to wish him "Happy New Year." Dan would be alone that day, all alone on the day of judgement and atonement. This situation was almost intolerable to me. This seemed to violate the heart of Judaism whose purpose is to bring people together as they face God.

I empathized with Dan about being on the ward on Yom Kippur. I told him I was unsure of my own plans to go to shul,* but I wouldn't be seeing my family as they live back East. We talked briefly about the importance of the holiday and of family. Then, I ran to my office to quell the strong feelings this conversation had evoked in me.

On Yom Kippur, I went to work. Dan and I briefly joked about the fact that we were both on the ward on this important day. Neither of us wanted to acknowledge this as a major sacrifice. I had, after all, chosen myself to go to work while Dan's choice was made for him. Nevertheless, both of us just wanted the day to pass quickly and to forget that it was Yom Kippur. Finally, the day was over.

I never did think of Dan the same way after that day. Somehow my perception of him shifted from patient first/Jewish second to Jewish first/patient second. Now, when he wished to speak Yiddish to me, it was my pleasure to listen. I explored his delusions about being a rabbi with him instead of challenging his impaired reality

---

*shul — synagogue (Yiddish expression).

testing. We discussed the importance of Judaism in his family, and the reasons for its prominence in his self-identification. I became actively involved in discussing his plan for discharge and voiced support for his plans to be discharged to a Jewish Board and Care home located in the center of the Los Angeles Jewish community.

My work with Dan on the ward began to reflect the changes in my overall approach. Something major had shifted in me — it was as if I had shed the self-protective layer that I had previously worn at work. I now called less on technique, and worked more openly with patients. I shared important aspects of my life more readily with patients when they asked. In short, I stopped hiding my personal attributes, trying less to be a "blank screen" and more to be a full human being.

In reflecting back over my work with Jewish patients, I wondered why Dan had struck the deepest chord with respect to my Jewish identity. In the past, I had worked with other psychotic Jewish patients (who also happened to be male) in intensive psychodynamically-oriented psychotherapy. I have come to realize that because I worked with Dan in group and milieu treatment, but not individually, I felt safer allowing my personal and cultural values to emerge, and did not hide behind a therapist persona. In my prior individual psychotherapy with psychotic male Jewish patients, I attempted to conceal my cultural and gender identifications in order to safeguard against exceedingly powerful transferences and countertransferences. My fear, perhaps irrational, was that my patients and I would be locked into stereotyped traditional Jewish male-female interactional patterns which would then interfere with the therapeutic work.

I remembered while writing this paper that there had been another Jewish doctor on the ward over the "high holidays."* Perhaps I had forgotten his presence because he and Dan did not discuss Judaism, nor did he and I acknowledge to each other that we were both at work on Yom Kippur. I also never discussed the significance of the events that took place between Dan and me with

---

*high holidays — The Jewish New Year holidays: Rosh Hashanah and Yom Kippur. The holidays involve a period of soul-searching and reflection in order to cleanse oneself for the new year.

this doctor even though he had a somewhat supervisory role over my work. In retrospect, it appears that while I had become a channel for therapeutic cultural explorations for Dan, the Jewish male doctor had not. This incongruity may reflect a difference in personal styles. But more importantly, I feel that it supports the feminist literature on gender difference, suggesting that women are better attuned and more comfortable with relational issues than men (Chodorow, 1974; Gilligan, 1982; Kaplan, 1984; Lerner, 1983; Miller, 1976, 1984; Stiver, 1984; Surrey, 1985). Perhaps Dan recognized this, and sought me out to meet a need that is usually met by women within traditional Jewish culture.

So, where do I go from here? I am now more aware of the power that shared religious commonalities can have within a therapeutic relationship and that I can call upon this positive force and use it effectively in my work when it feels appropriate. I also hope to raise my colleagues' awareness of Jewish issues so that they are better attuned to them and more adept at addressing Jewish dynamics as they surface on the ward. I have learned that being a Jewish woman places me simultaneously at an advantage and disadvantage as a therapist. The trick will be to value my gender-related and cultural strengths and struggle against the more odious, sexist role expectations placed on me. Finally, I have realized that "professionalism" had taken preeminence over my personal values both at work and in general. I had been more concerned with the work ethic than with my cultural and personal ethics. Next year on the high holidays, I plan to be at synagogue with my family and I hope that Dan will be at his synagogue, too.

REFERENCES

Chodorow, N. (1974). Family structure and feminine personality. In M. Rosaldo & L. Lamphere (Eds.), *Woman, culture and society* (pp.43-66). Stanford, CA: Standford University Press.

Gilligan, C. (1982). *In a different voice: Women's conception of self and morality*. Cambridge, MA: Harvard University Press.

Kaplan, A. (1984). The "self-in-relation": Implications for depression in women (Work in Progress Paper No. 84-03). Wellesley, MA: Wellesley College, The Stone Center.

Lerner, H.E. (1983). Female dependency in context: Some theoretical and technical considerations. *American Journal of Othopsychiatry, 53,* 697-705.

Miller, J.B. (1984). The development of women's sense of self (Work in Progress Paper No. 12). Wellesley, MA: Wellesley College, The Stone Center.

Miller, J.B. (1976). *Toward a new psychology of women.* Boston: Beacon Press.

Stiver, I.P. (1984). The meaning of "dependency" in female-male relationships (Work in Progress Paper No. 83-07). Wellesley, MA: Wellesley College, The Stone Center.

Surrey, J. (1985). The "self-in-relation": A theory of women's development (Work in Progress Paper No. 13). Wellesley, MA: Wellesley College, The Stone Center.

Yalom, I. (1983). *Inpatient group psychotherapy.* New York: Basic Books.

Anti-Semitism in the Therapy Room

Kayla Weiner

The issues surrounding anti-Semitism in therapy are complex. It is necessary for all therapists to become more knowledgeable about the reality of being Jewish in modern American culture in order to adequately address the needs of Jewish clients and to counter the forces of anti-Semitism. This paper raises issues of anti-Semitism, Jewish identity development, and mental health; dispels some myths and stereotypes; and provides a frame for helping therapists better understand Jewish clients.

What is the impact on the therapeutic relationship if a Jewish therapist identifies her Jewishness to her client? Is it OK to wear symbols of Jewishness or to take time off for religious holidays? What is the role of the Jewish therapist working with a Jewish client? How does a non-Jewish therapist address the issues of cultural identity with Jewish clients?

These are important issues to think about, and their solutions relate directly to the philosophy of the feminist therapist and how she runs her life and practice. Non-Jewish therapists may need to be educated to be able to address anti-Semitism within the therapeutic relationship. Jewish therapists may need to explore their own internalized Jewish experience and any possible unresolved issues about their own Jewish identity. Each clinician, Jew and non-Jew, must perform a personal inventory to better understand internalized hates, fears, and confusions about issues of Jewishness and must raise cultural issues with each Jewish client to unravel the client's Jewish life experience.

Kayla Weiner, PhD, is a Jewish woman in independent practice in Seattle, WA. In addition to her clinical work she has been speaking and writing for several years on the issues of Jewish women and anti-Semitism.

As a feminist therapist I believe my role is to provide a client with as much information as needed in order to allow the client to live a full and productive life. This includes the awareness that many of the problems individuals face in life, many of the wounds suffered, are not a result of their own doing or being, but are a part of the condition of living in a world which is oppressive to various groups. Therapists have an obligation to identify anti-Semitism and help each client understand the interrelationship of the various oppressions.

When discussing my fee increase, a non-Jewish client said, "I don't want to pay more. I guess it's the Jew in me." I found an appropriate time in the session to be clear and direct. I let the client know how the remark made me feel, how anti-Semitism affects society and how it affects her as an individual. A therapeutic issue for this client was how her attitudes toward Jews could affect her relationship with her Jewish son-in-law.

When a Jewish client makes an anti-Semitic remark or says something disparaging of Jews, it is necessary to explore the client's internalized oppression. Judith Weinstein Klein, in her book *Jewish Identity and Self Esteem* (1980, p. 6), states, "The conflict between assimilation and identification for Jews exacts a price in discontent, alienation, and various forms of self hate." She notes an avoidance and embarrassment at explicit attention to Jewishness. This conflict is a result of wanting to belong and be accepted by the dominant culture coupled with a desire or need for invisibility. Fear of discrimination and annihilation has yielded a tenacious and pervasive fear among Jews; history has taught us we do not have any long term safety (Weiner, 1988).

Being different is central to being Jewish. Often the color of our skin is different and there are certain physical features associated with being Jewish which we learn quickly are not within the acceptable norms of white society. Our food is different and our names are different and we are often considered strange, somehow out of touch, and of less value than the rest of society. The central impact of anti-Semitism turns being different into being treated as not as good. What does that mean to the psyche of the Jewish individual?

Psychoanalytic theory would suggest that the Jew is the obvious receptacle of the "bad me" and therefore serves a purpose for others in society. Within Jewish individuals, when the conflict between "good and bad me" is overwhelming, or when children experience themselves as passive victims, they may not be able to integrate the "bad-me" images into stable self-concepts. Some children may tend to dissociate negative self images and experience them as "not-me." Being a member of a minority group, especially a despised minority, often makes integration of negative self-images difficult and contributes to dissociation (Klein, 1980). This dynamic is responsible for the internalization of anti-Semitism by some Jews who see other Jews as the "bad me," and who say, "I'm not that (i.e., bad) kind of Jew."

There is often a desire to join the majority. The need to be included by the dominant culture may result in self-destructive attitudes and behavior. Identification with the aggressor must be understood as a self-protective coping mechanism to allow one to live within the dominant culture.

An example of this is reflected in the words of one of the subjects in Epstein's book, *Children of the Holocaust* (1982):

> I wanted to be a special kind of Jew, a Jew who wasn't too Jewish. I stayed observant but I didn't want to be conspicuous. I had this theory if people knew, I'd be one of the first to be taken away. I had very blond hair when I was young and I got very upset when it began to turn dark. When people would say, "you don't look Jewish," it made me happy. I thought I was safe. And when it turned darker I thought I'd never escape. (p. 42)

The Jewish child in school may be alienated because Jewish reality is often ignored; school activities on Friday night disregard the reality of the observant Jew — they exclude the Jewish child causing the child and family to feel and be perceived as "other." Important Jewish religious holidays such as Yom Kippur are slighted, while less important holidays such as Channukah are exaggerated to fit the need of the dominant culture. Jewish children are expected to honor Christian holidays. For many Jews, to be wished "Merry Christmas" is to deny their personal reality and uniqueness. The denial is similar to when men view women's issues as irrelevant, or heterosexuals are unaware of the needs of lesbians and gays. There are few role models for Jewish children in American history. Heidi Rechteger, a Jewish therapist from Los Angeles said, "I never related to George Washington or the Pilgrims. That was not my history and I knew it" (personal communication, 1989).

Jewish cultural illiteracy of the therapist is often a limiting factor in psychotherapy. It encompasses a failure to appreciate the historical and cultural context of Jewish experience; a failure to understand an individual's development of self when one grows up as "other"; and a failure to understand the internalized oppression — the owning of a negative self image by Jews and the effect of that image on thought and behavior.

I don't usually announce my ethnicity in my initial session, yet who I am becomes clear over time and within the therapeutic relationship. I often wear a Star of David or other symbols of my Jewishness and I make no appointments to see clients on major Jewish holidays. A clear statement of my Jewish identity provides a model for clients who are attempting to define themselves. In a sense, it gives clients permission to say who they are.

Jews are often judged for being "too pushy, too loud, too successful, or too rich." For Jews there is an historical reality of violence, oppression, and forced migration that teaches us we must be better and more if we want to be equal. It very early spurs getting ahead, hard work, discipline, achievement, and success. This striving for success combined with fear of repression often leads to a sense of insecurity. One child of Holocaust survivors noted, "There's a reluctance to accept success and be smug about it . . . my parents feel they can't be too secure . . ." (Epstein, 1982, p. 32). Another survivor noted that when she asked her mother why they never had tuna casserole like other people, her mother said she had gone three years without meat in the concentration camps (Epstein, 1982). Meat had become a symbol of security and achievement for her. The emphasis on security needs to be understood within the context of the experience of the current generation of Jews.

The concept of the Jewish mother as over-bearing, dominating and "enmeshed," to use the term of systems therapists, is demeaning and racist in that it fails to understand the gender structuring in the Jewish family. It denies the historical role of the Jewish woman in the shtetl (Jewish community in Europe). Her role was that of a strong and competent woman; her function was to do everything for the family at the expense of her own needs or desires (Siegel, 1986). In America her role remained the same and added the burden of work outside the home. When Jewish men were better able to provide financial support, they began restricting the work of the women and showering the women with material possessions as a sign of the men's accomplishments (Baum, Hyman & Michel, 1975). The image of the domineering, overprotective Jewish mother may be giving way to the equally unfavorable image of the "Jewish American Princess" (JAP), a woman who is supposedly pampered, materialistic, vain, self-centered and ambitious. The JAP stereotype often masks anti-Semitism (Henry & Taitz, 1988). The self image, as a result of the negative societal images, must be explored with each client.

Within the observant Jewish household, women's roles are often narrowly defined, limiting activities to homemaking and child-rearing. Henry and Taitz (1988, p. xiv) state, "We discovered that many of the limitations and restrictions on women's role which have been accepted in the Jewish society of Eastern Europe, were not necessarily the strictures of Jewish law, but evidence of prevailing social attitudes. There seemed to be a real confusion between what the Law said and what contemporary Jews assumed it said." Observant Jewish women must be helped to integrate their definition of womanhood in modern society with the definition of womanhood within their community.

Assimilation into the dominant culture may take the form of intermarriage. Vivien Benjamin of Jewish Family Service in Seattle noted (personal communication, 1989) that in some cases a Jewish man may marry a non-Jewish woman as a rejection of the "Jewish mother" whom he has learned to disparage as much as the rest of society, and then urge his wife to convert to Judaism so that his children can be raised Jewish. His desire to belong to the dominant culture and still retain a part of his heritage often results in a conflict when his wife converts and he ends up with exactly what he was attempting to reject. The attitude of many Jewish men toward their mothers has negatively affected the relationship between Jewish men and Jewish women.

Klein (1982) described a Jewish woman who complained in therapy that she could have intimacy but no sexual excitement with Jewish males, and sexual gratification but no intimacy with her non-Jewish partners. In a study conducted by the American Jewish Committee (1987) entitled *Jewish Women on the Way Up*, it was found that single women in the sample perceived Jewish men as more successful, intellectual, traditional and likely to be good fathers than non-Jewish men. However, they saw non-Jewish men as more macho, sexy and independent, and less self-absorbed than Jewish men. This lack of integration is damaging to the individual's sense of self and other and affects one's ability to bond.

The Jewish lesbian carries the burden of being triply oppressed, as woman, as Jew, and as lesbian, and must struggle all the more to develop an integrated identity.

The issues of inter-faith relationships must also be addressed in relation to the developmental task of individuation, a very difficult issue within Jewish culture which stresses that Jewish identity and family solidarity are related in a mutually supportive way.

There is an expectation within the Jewish family of closeness and connection. Verbit (1972), a therapist, remarks about having been told he had a "problem" because he often did things socially with his in-laws. Flo Kinsler, a Jewish therapist with Jewish Family Services in Los Angeles, recalled (personal communication, 1989) that she was told by a therapist there was something wrong with her because she spoke with her son once a week when he went away to college. Within the context of the Jewish family, as well as all families, frequent contact between parents and children could be viewed as normal and healthy rather than pathological. In Jewish parents, the need to know their children are healthy and, above all, safe, may reasonably be intensified by memories of the Holocaust when children were taken from parents never to be returned.

Jews are often chided for being "too serious" and not able to play; and many are accused of pathology instead of being appreciated and acknowledged for being involved in multiple social change activities. The child of a Holocaust survivor spoke of his respect for his parents. He felt that being their child had given him a certain depth, a seriousness about life that most people don't have. He was aware of evil in the world and felt required to actively struggle to prevent a revival of the sort of thing that led to the murder of his family (Epstein, 1982). *Tikkun Olum*, "to heal, repair and transform the world," is a basic philosophy of Judaism which *requires* each Jew to make the world a better place. Criticism for social action is another way in which the Jew is set in conflict between cultural/religious/family values and dominant societal values.

An intense need to acquire an education is often a part of the Jewish psyche. From biblical times, scholarship was valued above all else. More recently the striving for education has been related to self-sufficiency. It is often said within Jewish homes that a person can lose everything, but what's inside the head cannot be taken away.

Jews value the ability to articulate their thoughts as a by-product of learning, and use argument as a method for the development of rational thought (McGoldrick, Pearce & Giordano, 1982). The expression of intense emotion is also characteristic of Jewish culture yet it is little understood or appreciated in white, middle class, Christian America and rarely is it considered a virtue. Questioning is a basic premise of the religion. The ancient rabbis questioned all laws of G-d and human; modern Jews continue to do so. An in-joke among Jews: "Why do Jews ask so many questions?" The response, "Why not?" While others often perceive this questioning and debate as dissension, Jews perceive it as seeking the truth.

I have heard horror stories of Holocaust survivors being in treatment for 17 years without ever having their war time issues addressed (Danieli, personal communication, 1989). Too often the issues of the Jewish client are not understood or even addressed simply because the therapist does not know that ethnic issues are involved. It is necessary for the therapist to make every effort to become knowledgeable about an individual's culture. If an issue arises which seems confusing to the clinician, there may be a cultural component. It is totally appropriate to inquire about the ethnic or religious context of the client's internal experience. Why, you may wonder, is it such a big deal that the client cannot go home for the Passover? If you ask, you will learn that for many Jews, Passover has the emotional power that Christmas has for many non-Jews. It is a time of ritual, a time of connection with family and historical roots.

Ethnotherapy is a powerful tool to be used with the Jewish client. Klein (1982, p. 10) states that "Ethnotherapy seeks to move people from conflicts in their identity to a more secure and positive grounding in their group, as well as a more positive self-esteem. Personal problems are then seen through an ethnic lens in their defining social context."

Many issues remain to be explored. Should Jewish clients be urged to work only with Jewish therapists? How does a non-observant Jewish therapist relate to an Orthodox Jew or vice versa? An in depth analysis of the Jewish attitude toward gender and gender roles and their effect on Jewish women is also critical. My hope and intent here has been to begin that process of exploration, to provide a general sense of the experience of being Jewish in the world, to examine how anti-Semitism affects the Jewish psyche, and to provide some direction for making our role as therapists, Jew and non-Jew, more responsive to the needs of our clients.

REFERENCES

Baum, C., Hyman, P., & Michel, S. (1975). *The Jewish woman in America*. NY: New American Library.

Epstein, H. (1982). *Children of the Holocaust*. NY: Penguin.

Henry, S., & Taitz, E. (1988). *Written out of history: Our Jewish foremothers*. NY: Biblio Press.

Weinstein Klein, J. (1982). *Jewish identity and self-esteem*. NY: American Jewish Committee.

McGoldrick, M., Pearce, J., & Giordana, J. (1982). *Ethnicity and family therapy*. NY: Guilford.

Monson, R.G. (1987). *Jewish women on the way up*. NY: American Jewish Committee.

Siegel, R.J. (1986). Anti-semitism and sexism in stereotypes of Jewish women. In D. Howard, (Ed.), *Dynamics of feminist therapy*. NY: Haworth Press.

Verbit, M. (1972). Contemporary Jewish identity and family dynamics. *Jewish Heritage*: Summer 72, 47-53.

Weiner, K. (1988). *Women and anti-Semitism*. Paper presented at the Association for Women in Psychology conference, Bethesda, Md.

View 5338